Land Your Dream Job Anywhere

The Complete Mac's List Guide To Finding Work You Can Love

Land Your Dream Job Anywhere

The Complete Mac's List Guide To Finding Work You Can Love

First Edition

Mac's List • 620 SW Fifth Avenue, Suite 702 • Portland, OR 97204

Land Your Dream Job Anywhere

The Complete Mac's List Guide To Finding Work You Can Love

Publisher: Mac's List
President: Mac Prichard
Managing Director: Ben Forstag
Community Manager: Jenna Forstrom
Finance Manager: Anneka Winters
Administrative Assistant: Jessica Black
Editorial and Production Manager: Kris Swanson, Swanson Editorial Services
Design and Layout: Hilary Hudgens and Sarah Reed, Hilary Hudgens Design
Photos: CanStock; RF123
Copyeditor: Tanya Hanson
Proofreader: Margaret Hines

ISBN: 978-0-9909551-3-9

Mac's List
620 SW Fifth Avenue, Suite 702 • Portland, Oregon 97204 • USA
Mac's List's mission is to help people throughout the country
find rewarding, interesting jobs that pay decent salaries
and to help employers find the best possible
candidates for those jobs.

Table of Contents

Introduction

Anyone who has ever gone through a job search knows that it can be a frustrating, dispiriting, and painful experience.

As in. . . root canal painful.

I know this because I've gone through several extended periods of unemployment in my life. I also speak with countless people each year who are in the midst of difficult job searches.

For most job hunters the whole process seems mysterious and opaque. They follow the seemingly straightforward rules—find a job online, apply, wait—with little success. In fact, the number one complaint I hear from job seekers is that they send out dozens of applications and rarely get any response from employers, not even a rejection notice.

This process can be soul-crushing, even for the most accomplished, confident professional. It's hard not to internalize this inability to connect with employers. Many job seekers end up wondering, "What's wrong with me?"

But here's the truth. . . For most people the "problem" isn't within themselves. The problem is almost entirely with their job search strategy.

Most people are never taught how to look for a job. High school and college teach us the technical skills to use in our career, but we are never taught the nuts-and-bolts of how to conduct a strategic job search. Instead, we are left mostly to rely on trial and error.

That's the reason this book exists—to outline a proven job-search strategy that actually works. In the pages that follow, you'll find a process that results in a faster, less-frustrating job search and maximizes your chances of finding a job you love.

Job hunting is not an innate ability; no one is born with the magical power to land a great job. It is a learned skill that anyone can master with practice. I know this because I used to struggle with finding meaningful work opportunities. Fortunately, in my mid-twenties I met a career advisor at Northeastern University who showed me how to network with professionals and find amazing jobs.

Following her advice has helped me land several dream jobs. It's how I came to work for a human rights group that took members of Congress on foreign fact-finding trips. It's how I got a plum job as a communications director for a Portland mayoral candidate. And it's how I became a speechwriter for the governor of Oregon.

In 2001 I founded Mac's List, an online community for jobseekers looking for meaningful work opportunities. I wanted to share practical and actionable career advice to help people find work they love. What started out as a simple listserv with a few dozen followers has since grown into a diversified, full-time business. Today, my staff and I operate a daily blog, a weekly podcast, regular networking events, and a library of online courses. We also run one of the largest and most successful regional job boards in the country. Nearly 80,000 people use Mac's List each month as part of their job search.

This book combines the best information from the Mac's List blog, along with job-hunting tips from national experts who have participated in my podcast, Find Your Dream Job. It provides a chapter-by-chapter guide to finding work, as well as tips for managing your career into the future.

Whether you're reading this book as a prelude to your job hunt or as a tool to reinvigorate a stalled search, you'll find all the information you need to kickstart the process. I applaud you for making the investment of time and energy to learn a new, better way to find work. I'm confident this investment will pay big dividends in the not-so-distant future.

Mac Prichard
Founder and Publisher
Mac's List

Acknowledgments

On behalf of the entire Mac's List team, I'd like to thank all the people who have contributed to the development of this book.

Our success begins, most fundamentally, with the support and feedback we get from the Mac's List community—the more than 80,000 people who interact with us online, via social media, and at networking events each month. We get so many great ideas and suggestions from our followers. Your job-search needs and challenges shape the topics we write about every day. Thank you for your trust and support. We couldn't do this without you!

Special thanks go to the national job search and career advancement experts who contributed content to this book: Melissa Anzman, Farai Chideya, Hallie Crawford, Jennie Day-Burget, Aubrie De Clerck, Jenny Foss, Chris Guillebeau, Kerry Hannon, Gabrielle Nygaard, Nathan Perez, Deena Pierott, Don Raskin, Dawn Rasmussen, Joshua Waldman, Jeff Weiss, and Kirsten Wyatt. These people are true authorities in their respective fields and I'm honored to share page space with them!

Many thanks, as well, to everyone who has contributed to the the Mac's List blog, which is the basis for this book. This includes current and former staff of Mac's List and Prichard Communications, as well as our many interns and guest bloggers! Your submissions and editorial expertise have helped position Mac's List as a trusted job search resource.

We are particularly indebted to our editorial and design team, who took a collection of rough manuscripts (some hand-written on yellow legal pads) and turned it into a beautiful, polished book. A big thank you goes out to writer and editor Kris Swanson of Swanson Editorial Services, who managed this process and didn't get too upset when we were late on deadlines; designers Hilary Hudgens and Sarah Reed of Hilary Hudgens Design, who crafted an elegant book even if though we tried to mess it up; copyeditor Tanya Hanson, who won't let us split infinitives; and proofreader Margaret (Peggy) Hines, who was our last line of defense against dreaded typos!

And, of course, we need to thank you, the reader of this book! Without you, all of this work would be for naught. We'd love to hear what you think about the book. Please contact me at mac@macslist.org and let me know what's on your mind.

Mac Prichard and the Mac's List Team

1 Assessing Your Interests and Skills

---

*Before you can find the perfect job, you need to take a good, hard look
at yourself, your loves and hates, and your strengths and weaknesses.
Begin by ridding yourself of any preconceived ideas you might have about
what you should do (or what others think you should do) and invest the time
in exploring your passions and how you can apply them to your job search.*

Do the analytical work.

There's no way around it. You've got to do the work if you want an honest self-assessment. Whether you are looking for your first job, searching for a new job, or changing careers, you need to commit to this task and remember that time and effort now will save time and effort down the line.

For most people, the key to happiness in any career is to find a workplace that shares their values and a job that allows them to use their strengths. So the question is, where to begin?

Take advantage of existing resources. Luckily, many tools and informational materials exist to help you answer these questions. Here are three of our favorites at Mac's List.

- *Strengths Finder 2.0* by **Tom Rath**: Do you ever wonder why you sometimes finish a day feeling exhausted and depleted, yet other days you walk away with a strong sense of self-worth and satisfaction of a job well done? According to Rath, on the exhausted days, you probably didn't get to use your strengths. On the days when you were in the flow, you were able to use your talents toward a job well done. This book teaches you how to identify those strengths. (Bonus: If you buy the book, you get an access code to take an online assessment, which takes about thirty minutes.)

- *What Color Is Your Parachute? A Practical Manual for Job Hunters and Career Changers* by **Richard Bolles:** Yes, it was first published in 1970 and has had more than forty editions since then, but it still remains an invaluable tool for professional self-discovery. Doing the exercises helps to uncover new ideas and to reveal potential areas for informational interviews, exploration, and research. It's a great career guide and self-discovery tool all in one.

- *The Career Guide for Creative and Unconventional People* by **Carol Eikleberry:** Exploring your strengths can lead you down different career paths, so you may need to get creative in your search for happiness at work. This book can help you identify opportunities that you may never have thought of.

Ask yourself the hard questions. Is quality of life more important to you than a large paycheck? Do you hate teamwork? Do you love networking or dislike sitting in an office? Do you want to do different things every day? What are your passions? What are your values? Where do you see yourself in five years? In ten years? Do you not see a career path at all? An honest self-assessment gives you the opportunity to reflect on your answers to these and similar questions.

The Simple Formula for the Work You Were Born to Do: Joy–Money–Flow

by **Chris Guillebeau**, Author of *Born for This* and *The $100 Startup*

One tenet of traditional career advice is that everyone is different and we all want different things. It's true that every individual has a unique set of skills and interests, and that our backgrounds and contexts are naturally different. But do we all truly want different things? Maybe it's not so complicated: for the most part, we all want to find a career that meets the same few specific needs.

Despite our differences, most of us want a balanced life full of work that brings happiness and prosperity. As much as possible, we want to do something we enjoy. We want to put our skills to good use. And ideally, we don't want to face a false choice between love and money—we'd like to do what we love and be well compensated for it.

Put simply, here's what we are looking for:

- Something that makes us happy (joy)
- Something that's financially viable (money)
- Something that maximizes our unique skills (flow)

There's more than one path to this ideal world, but without all of these characteristics being met, you won't have a perfect match. It's entirely possible to do something you love that doesn't pay well. It's also possible to get paid well for something you dislike, or something you just tolerate—plenty of people essentially forge a compromise over putting up with a bad situation in exchange for a good paycheck. Finally, it's also possible to enjoy what you do or get paid well for it (or both), but to still lack the sense of all-encompassing flow, where the hours pass like minutes because you're so completely in the zone of doing something you're really good at.

None of those situations is what you want, though. To find the work you were born to do, you need the right combination of joy, money, and flow.

(Excerpted from *Born for This: How to Find the Work You Were Meant to Do*)

Wander with intention. "Not all who wander are lost," and, as Chris Guillebeau mentions above, sometimes the journey off the beaten path may turn out to be more rewarding than the one that follows a straight line. So don't get too hung up on having to move directly from point A to point B. The main thing is to continue the journey and be mindful about your experiences. If you follow your inclinations with deliberate thought and analysis, you will learn a lot about yourself along the way.

Explore your strengths and weaknesses in other ways. Sometimes a more tangential approach can yield productive insights and results.

- Many cities and regions have yoga, meditation, and higher-learning centers nearby. These can be great places for a weekend workshop, a relaxing day of reflection, or an inspirational nature getaway.
- Writing workshops can help unleash your creativity and foster self-reflection. Most major cities offer a variety of formal and informal options.
- Volunteer service programs are available through many organizations that offer volunteer opportunities in exchange for room and board.

- Travel with a purpose can help build self-knowledge, especially when you connect with organizations that combine travel and volunteer opportunities.

- Community classes can broaden your horizons and help you explore new realms. Most community colleges offer great and inexpensive opportunities for creative learning as well as career assessment and development.

Pay attention to other emotions and opinions.

While you think, reflect, and analyze, you also need to listen. What are your emotions, your actions, and your friends and family telling you? Don't tune them out. Instead, try to see what you can learn.

Get Fired Up About Finding Your Passion

by Jenna Forstrom, Community Manager at Mac's List

There are few things in the world that I get really, really excited about. (I'm talking kid-in-a-candy-shop excited.) They are: craft beer, serving the homeless, and my dog, Bullet. Although I know it's hard to believe, I'm also super passionate about my job.

I'm fascinated by how technology changes consumer behavior. I love using social media as a storytelling tool. The icing on the cake is that every day I get to help people find their dream jobs.

What is your light-up, crazy, can-talk-about-it-for-hours passion? I've discussed this with friends, job seekers, and employers for years. Here are my three go-to questions to help you figure out your passions.

Ask your family and friends, "What am I good at?" This is a great way to start your discovery process. Chances are your people—those closest to you—see a lot of great things about you that you might not recognize in yourself. Listen to their outside perspective! It might help you identify your passions—and it can be a huge emotional pick-me-up when you are looking for a job or thinking about making a career pivot.

Look at your calendar (or journal). Where do you spend your time? I've been saying all year, "I want to learn Khmer," but have I gone to a single lesson (or even signed up for a class)? Nope! Looking at your calendar and seeing what you actually spend time doing is a good way to figure out your passion. Are you a social butterfly or do you tend to spend more time alone or in small groups doing things like reading or painting?

Ask yourself, "How do I want to be remembered?" I know it's morbid to think about, but at some point you aren't going to be here anymore. What do you want to be known for? I call this my legacy plan. Every few months, I reflect on what I think my family, friends, and coworkers would say if I died. How would people remember me? My service to the community? My constant questions about after-work or weekend activities? My work on a project that went viral? How does that make me feel? Is that how I want to be remembered? If not, what changes do I need to make?

Spend some time answering these questions. Talk to your friends and family and make a list. You'll be surprised by what bubbles to the top. Once you see what emerges, you can start incorporating these passions into your job search. You can do it! We're all rooting for you!

Following Chris's advice and answering Jenna's questions can help you identify your passions. But how do you manage your fears and negative emotions during this process?

If you are doing an open and honest self-assessment, you are also opening a Pandora's box. Some of the emotions that fly out will be negative ones. Acknowledge them and deal with them openly and directly by doing the following:

- **Be kind to yourself.** According to the Dalai Lama, "If you want others to be happy, practice compassion. If you want to be happy, practice compassion." Kindness and self-acceptance are both the means and the end. Sometimes life just doesn't work out like we hoped it would. You graduate from college and it takes six months to find a paid gig. You second-guess getting your MBA instead of traveling. We all have decisions we regret and mistakes we've made. Stop beating yourself up; it's unproductive and self-defeating. Accept where you are right now in the present moment.

- **Be mindful and accept uncertainty.** Suffering stems from the stories we tell ourselves, our attachments and aversions, and our inability to accept uncertainty. We cling to the past because it's a known entity, and we try to predict and plan for the future to alleviate uncertainty. Accept the uncertainty that is the job search by bringing your attention to the present moment. Drop your awareness into the here and now. Be in the moment. Pet your dog. Meditate. Run. Hike. Surf. Whatever you do, do it with your whole heart and your whole attention. This will allow for the anxiety to soften and the bigger picture to unfold.

- **Be your own friend.** This means treating yourself as you would a best friend. Notice how you talk to yourself. Would you speak that way to a loved one? Not very likely, is it? Give yourself support, the same way you would a close friend. In the end, wherever you go, there you are, so learn to be kind to yourself because you are your own best ally. If you made a mistake, take mental note of what you'll do differently next time and forgive yourself for that mistake.

- **Be active.** Whatever form of exercise you enjoy, make room for it in your schedule. Regular exercise clears your head and elevates your mood.

- **Be generous with your time.** Put your skills to good use and show others what you can do by volunteering. You will come away with new energy as well as terrific contacts, excellent references, and great work samples. And thinking about others will take you outside yourself while giving you a different perspective on your world (and theirs).

Build a community based on your interests.

It's fun and motivational to share your passions and interests with others, and you are also creating a community of like-minded people who can inform and support your job search along the way.

Seek out others who share your interests. Volunteer or join a Meetup group. Go to a networking event. If you like Frisbee, join an Ultimate team. In need of relaxation and contemplation? Find a yoga studio that feels like home. Whatever it is, make sure it is something you are passionate about or are interested in exploring.

Support those connections. Connect with others, connect your new friends with old friends, and connect their friends with your friends. Support your community and it will support you.

Start something. Don't wait for others to act or to be chosen. Post an announcement on Meetup, ask to make an announcement at the monthly meeting of a professional group, or publish a manifesto on your blog. You may be amazed by who responds.

Creating community is especially important for job seekers in transition, such as recent college graduates, people returning to the workforce after raising children, or anyone who is trying to break into a new career field. Satya Byock, a Portland, Oregon, psychotherapist who specializes in working with young adults, offers several ways that you can draw strength from your community while weathering this life change.

- **Acknowledge to others that you are in transition.** This is especially important if you aren't sure where you are headed. Find a way to speak about your transition with confidence, which will give the helpful people in your network the opportunity to offer their support and ideas.
- **Create an accountability group.** Convene with others who are in similar situations to share your goals. Encourage discussion and supportive ideas. Have someone take notes. Try to focus on small goals you can accomplish in a short period of time. Then meet again in two weeks so you can all check on the progress you have made.

Put it all together.

The other goal of self-analysis is to take a good, clear-eyed look at your skills and see how they align with your interests and passions. When you are able to merge what you are good at with the things that you care about, you are well on your way to finding meaningful and productive work—in short, your ideal job.

Use Analysis to Turn Paralysis into Action!

by **Hallie Crawford,** Certified Career Coach
and Owner of HallieCrawford.com

Each year I meet with hundreds of people who are struggling to find a great, engaging job. I use two exercises to help these people analyze themselves and craft their ideal career model.

First I have them build a "career contrast list." This involves writing a list of items that answer the question: "What do I want to have in the ideal job?" They can base their answers on a current position ("What do I like and what do I dislike?") or on previous positions or classes ("What have I liked in the past and what have I not liked?"). The goal is simply to come up with a list of wants.

What's interesting about this activity is that it's not rocket science; in fact, it serves to show the jobseeker that they've known the answer all along. Seeing this list of likes and dislikes in black and white makes a huge difference for people. They realize that, (1) there may not be as many problematic factors in their current career path as they thought; and (2) it helps them be much more rational and practical about what they need to do next and what might work.

The second exercise is to walk clients through an ideal career model to identify what is most rewarding and fulfilling for them. We explore their career values. (What are your values in your job? Where do you find meaning?) We focus on enjoyment. (What else would you like to do?) We have them identify the talents and skills they want to leverage in their ideal job. (What have you liked in the past? Are you qualified for the dream job you're considering?) We also dive into each client's education, personality type, previous work environments, and compensation expectations. The goal is to make this analysis as complete as possible—a comprehensive 360-degree review of their career wants and needs.

This may sound like a lot of work. And, in truth, it is! But my biggest piece of advice is "Just take action now." I know that sounds kind of simple, but too many people call me a year later and say, "Hey, I talked to you before and I haven't done anything about this because I got scared." I tell people to just break it down into small chunks. Start with that first list, the list of wants. Just start there. Spend thirty minutes on it. Get the ball rolling and know that it will unfold for you over time. The sooner you start, the better.

Address your weaknesses by polishing your skills.

Once you've finished your self-assessment and have a better understanding of your passions, your dislikes, your skills, and your strengths and weaknesses, it's a good time to see how your skills meet the needs of the marketplace. What does today's job market demand of qualified applicants? How many of those skills do you already have? What others do you need to acquire?

Many recruiters and hiring professionals tend to divide skills loosely into hard skills (tangible skills that can be easily learned) and soft skills (more intangible skills that relate to how people interact in the workplace).

Master these hard skills. Kimberlee Stiens, a blogger and editorial coordinator for Vox.com, recommends the following skills because they apply to many kinds of jobs in many different areas. Do you have them? Do you need them?

- **Coding:** The marketplace rewards those who understand and can perform basic HTML and CSS coding. With a beginner's knowledge, you can tweak a website, customize a blog, or make adjustments to online images.

- **Graphic design:** In many offices, some employees double as graphic designers who can work in programs such as InDesign and Photoshop. If you can modify a photo, create a rate card, build a professional binder, and so on, you can do simple design projects on your own.

- **Public speaking:** Scared of speaking in front of others? Join a group like Toastmasters International that allows you to practice in front of a supportive group and build your confidence.

- **Writing:** Good writers are keepers in the workforce. Learn to write for the web and social media so that you are concise and practiced in the art of engaging others, and you'll be a success at your new job.

- **Advanced Excel:** Many of us play "phone a friend" when it comes to Excel. How about you? How many times have you looked at Excel and thought, "If only I knew how to merge and sort these files?" Get rid of Excel anxiety and take a class. Your new employer will be impressed and your friends will thank you.

Work toward acquiring soft skills. These skills are harder to pinpoint, but their very subtlety is what makes them so valuable in the workplace. Potential employers pick up on soft skills through nonverbal cues, previous accomplishments, and references from people they know. In fact, many readers tell us that they found work from relationships that they cultivated and from people in their network. How many of the following soft skills do you have? How many do you need to acquire?

- **Maintaining relationships:** People hire people they know or who are recommended to them by people they trust. Word of mouth is key in many businesses. To get trusted recommendations, a company or organization must have good and trusted relationships with colleagues and customers. Their future success depends on finding employees who know how to do this, too.

- **Working in teams:** Today's workplace demands collaboration. Businesses highly value staff members who work well with others, especially across different organizations, and so do their clients.

- **Staying flexible:** For many American workers, the era of big, bureaucratic organizations is over. Even at large companies, priorities can change quickly. Today's customers expect organizations to be nimble and able to turn on a dime.

- **Learning:** These days everyone has to be a lifelong learner. Job candidates who join professional groups, attend webinars and workshops, and monitor the latest newsletters and blogs stand out and impress potential hirers.

- **Listening:** Sometimes people—colleagues or customers—don't know what they want or have trouble explaining a need or idea. One of the most valuable assets any company can have is staff who know how to listen to others, draw people out, and help everybody understand each other. Divas and monologists? Not so useful.

Stay current. Every year, major trend forecasters predict the most critical skill sets for the coming year. Stay up to date with these lists and keep your job-hunting skills fresh. Meghan Casserly at *Forbes* magazine identified ten skills the Career Builder website identified as key. Note that they are a mix of both hard and soft skills: critical thinking, complex problem solving, judgment and decision making, active listening, computers and electronics, mathematics, operations and systems analysis, monitoring, programming, and sales and marketing.

Dig deeper!

For links to some of the topics covered in this chapter (including mindfulness, essential workplace skills, self-kindness and success, and career transitions, among many), go to www.macslist.org/references.

2 Understanding and Using Online and Social Media

Before you begin contacting and networking with people as part of your job search, make sure your online house is in order. You need to be virtually visible, but only in the best way possible. Do an audit of your online presence and work to eliminate the negative while accentuating the positive. Along the way you'll acquire new skills, such as using social media, joining professional networking websites, and practicing online etiquette.

Clean up your act.

Looking for a job? "You should take care that your social media personality won't kill your job prospects," says career coach Melissa Anzman, of the *Launch Yourself* blog. Employers have admitted long ago that they check out job applicants online as part of the hiring process.

In spite of this common hiring practice, many people say and do things on the internet that could hurt their next job search. Consider your Twitter feed, Instagram profile, Facebook page, and Vine accounts as places where people can get a sense of your personality, all without ever having met you or spoken to you in person. Here's how to make sure that they get a good first impression, not a bad one.

Think like an employer. Do what every human resource manager does: search your name and see what turns up. Then drill down. Although most people don't go beyond the first page of organic search results, you can't always count on this. Don't just search your name; search any previous names, nicknames, or other handles that could be traced back to you. You might be surprised by what pops up.

Don't limit yourself to Google. Use Bing, too, and visit the social networking sites where you have accounts as well as the websites and blogs where you've written under your own name. Clear your browser's data or open a private or "incognito" window to see what a stranger would see when viewing your online identity. Does the material reflect what you want an employer to think about you? Look at your digital footprint from the perspective of a potential employer.

Clean up your online profile. Take action when you find unflattering material. Remove tags from Facebook photos and posts that you don't want shared. Do the same with other social media sites and online platforms. If you can't delete the content yourself, write to the owner of the account, blog, or website, and ask him or her to do it for you. Do your utmost to have it made private or deleted, but be polite about it—shooting off an irritated email could backfire.

Strengthen your privacy settings. Privacy settings for social media accounts can be complicated. Take the time to master them. Privacy options seem not only to change every two weeks but to get more complex. Check your visibility settings often and then check them twice to ensure your online accounts present a positive public image.

Think ahead. Next time, resist the urge to post that rant or send that dicey Snapchat. Consider adding a respected mentor (a judgmental relative will work in a pinch) to your social networks to keep your future posts in line. "When in doubt, leave it out" is the golden rule for maintaining a squeaky-clean online presence.

Polish your online presence.

Once you get rid of as much of the bad as you can, it's time to improve your online persona.

Use SEO tactics to push down the bad news and raise the good. Sometimes you can't make embarrassing content go away, but you can make it harder to find with simple search engine optimization (SEO) techniques. Try to solve the problem yourself before you turn to the booming online reputation management industry. Easy tactics include blogging on professional topics and completing personal profiles for different social media services. As Mac Prichard, Mac's List founder and president of Prichard Communications, says, "Take it from someone who's never had the luxury of hiding behind a common name: there's only so much you can do to wipe yourself off the face of the web. At that point, go on the offensive. Create a professional website, blog, or Twitter account, and start putting out material you'd want employers to see."

Make sure you have a robust online presence. In today's workplace, you must be found digitally in multiple places to maintain a level of professional credibility. If you can't be found online, employers will assume you haven't kept up with the times. Be involved with blogs in your field, whether as a writer or a named commenter. Starting your own blog, Facebook group, or website will help boost your online presence in a positive way.

Create an attractive online personality. According to a CareerBuilder survey, more than one-third of employers (thirty-seven percent) now use social networks to screen potential job candidates. Maintaining your online persona is one of the newer skills that job seekers must possess. Use this opportunity to show multiple aspects of your experience and personality, both professional and personal. Your passions make you an attractive employee in the eyes of potential employers—just make sure all the interests and hobbies you mention are neutral and unlikely to offend.

Stay active online. It's not enough to burst online with a flurry of social media pages, blog posts, and online commentary. You have to update regularly and keep yourself current. Remember, in online time, a month of silence is like disappearing forever. Frequent posts and updates keep you visible and alive in people's minds.

Use online resources to promote your professional identity.

Polishing and enhancing your online presence is a great way to market yourself to potential employers. One of the best ways is to make use of the many available online tools and resources that can help you increase that presence while connecting with other people.

Use LinkedIn. This professional networking website is the granddaddy of all online job search resources. One of the most common requests received from Mac's List readers is: "How can I build a LinkedIn profile to catch the attention of a recruiter or an employer?"

It's a question you should ask yourself, even if you're not looking for work. Think about what an employer will see when your own LinkedIn page pops up on Google. Your LinkedIn account is more than an online resume or a place to check for job postings. Many professionals now use the site to learn about new coworkers, potential vendors, or possible business partners. Others rely on LinkedIn to share news and ideas with colleagues, customers, and employers.

In a recent survey by Jobvite of more than 1,000 human resource and recruiting professionals, ninety-three percent of respondents say they use LinkedIn to find the right candidate.

LinkedIn has more than 430 million members and is growing rapidly, adding new users at the rate of two per second. How can you stand out in such a crowded community and attract the attention of those you want to know about your accomplishments and abilities? Take the following steps:

- **Show yourself.** A profile page without your picture looks forgotten and stagnant. Pick a good photo. This is your first impression, so make it the right one. As Jeff Haden writes in "6 Steps to a More Marketable LinkedIn Profile" in *Inc.* magazine, "The best photo strikes a balance between professionalism and approachability, making you look good but also real." Don't post a vacation photo. Keep it professional. If you can't afford a studio portrait, ask a friend to take a simple headshot with your smartphone.
- **List all key jobs.** Don't add every part-time gig or summer job you've ever had, but do include the most important and relevant jobs in your career. And don't limit yourself to your current position—a common mistake.
- **Showcase your work.** Did you know that LinkedIn will allow you to link to your websites and your Twitter handle as well as stream recent posts from your WordPress blog? Do you have projects you want to showcase? Use the "Projects" feature of LinkedIn. While most of us have posted a career summary on LinkedIn, "Projects" features your special skills. Be sure to use it to highlight your work.
- **Emphasize results, not duties.** The best resumes describe what a person has accomplished, not just his or her responsibilities. The same is true on LinkedIn. In the "Summary" and "Experience" sections of your profile, talk about the benefits you produced for an employer and include keywords that recruiters may use when searching for candidates.
- **Use the "Skills and Endorsements" section strategically.** You can include up to fifty skills and collect endorsements for each of them from your LinkedIn connections. Think strategically about the strengths you want others to know

that you have, and add them now yourself. Don't wait for your LinkedIn connections to add them for you.

- **Ask for endorsements (and give them).** A short two- or three-sentence endorsement from a former supervisor or colleague adds invaluable credibility to your profile. Aim to have at least one endorsement for each job. Also offer to give endorsements to others you know well and whose work you can recommend.

- **Build your network every day.** Don't limit your LinkedIn connections to current or recent coworkers. The larger your network, the easier it is for you to connect with employers and leaders in your field. Add colleagues from past jobs, instructors and students from college and high school, and friends, neighbors, and others you know socially. LinkedIn is also a good way to connect with people you meet professionally. Most people are willing to accept invitations from those they haven't met if they share common professional interests.

- **Send a personal note when connecting.** As Jenny Foss, of JobJenny.com writes in "Your LinkedIn Intervention: 5 Changes You Must Make" in *Forbes* magazine, "Avoid the default text like the plague. Make it personal. Make it specific. Make it clear that you're not the laziest person alive." Also, check the chapter resource list for a list of four tips that career expert Joshua Waldman, founder of CareerEnlightenment.com, has for connecting with strangers on LinkedIn.

- **Create a custom URL to publicize your LinkedIn profile.** This tip comes courtesy of Mara Woloshin, principal at Woloshin Communications, Inc. As she points out, the use of a consistent name across all your social networks builds personal brand awareness.

- **Join a group to engage with others and give back.** LinkedIn has become a popular publishing platform to share business ideas. Set aside time to review your news feed and comment on information your connections have posted. Post your own material, including professional milestones, events you plan to attend, or blog posts you've written. Visit and participate in LinkedIn groups. Take the time to explore and join some today!

Why You Need to Use LinkedIn as a Publishing and Blogging Platform

by **Joshua Waldman**, Founder of CareerEnlightenment.com

Using LinkedIn for publishing has really exploded over the last year. When you can tell your story with your voice—whether it's an article you write or someone else's work you are sharing along with your comments—it makes you a more rounded individual. You're not just another lifeless corporate profile on LinkedIn. You actually have something to say.

One of the reasons LinkedIn is such a great blogging platform is that posts tend to generate a lot of reader feedback. I get comments on my LinkedIn blog every week. Building this kind of community and dialog can be a huge asset in your job search. You want to be seen as a thought leader. Even if you aren't actively looking for a job, consistently publishing on LinkedIn helps you build your reputation bit by bit.

How do you get started? The first step is to start sharing. You don't have to publish a 500-word article right off the bat. Share an article someone else has written along with some of your own commentary on the topic. This is a great way to create engagement in your network. When you post, other people in your network will see it on their home page when they log in to LinkedIn. If they share it or like it or comment on it, your posts now get exposed to their networks. It's a simple way of growing your personal brand.

If not used to its full capacity, LinkedIn can be very passive. Many people just go online and tweak their profiles, and hope something will happen. That approach is disempowering and unproductive. Instead, you need to put yourself out there, and blogging is a good way to do that. Just as your profile should be engaging and tell your story, the content you publish is another way to create points of contact with your connections and position yourself in their opinions. There's no better way for people (including prospective employers) to see how you can provide value.

Explore other online professional resources. You can also use online tools to help you create a personal website, maintain and update a professional bio, or build a portfolio of your work. You can even take advantage of online resume-building services to help you polish your resume within an inch of its life. (See Chapter 5 for more on personal websites, portfolios, and resumes.)

Add social media to your job-hunting skills.

Like it or not, social media is here to stay. What does this mean for you? If you aren't participating in the conversation, you are definitely missing potential opportunities. Employing social media tactics to aid in your job search is an increasingly smart way to spend your time. Today, social media plays an important role in the decision process for hiring managers.

In addition to using social media to create and enhance your online persona, here are ways to make it a part of your job search.

Demonstrate your social media skills. As companies integrate and grow with social media, knowledge of the platforms will become a desired skill set. Social media can be used in a variety of ways and is great for networking in many types of careers.

Use social media to network. Networking isn't new, and it's the best way to find a job. Social networks have taken the barriers out of contacting and connecting with those in hiring positions. Follow the websites, social networking pages, and company blogs of employers you admire so that you know more about them when you connect with them later.

Inquiries don't have to be formal and can revolve around common interests. Learn to love Twitter (even if you don't already). It is estimated that more than 313 million people are now using Twitter. Take advantage of its reach and create a Twitter strategy for your job search by following these tips:

- **Use advanced search and know the hashtags for your job search.** Joshua Waldman recommends going to search.twitter.com and performing an advanced search for the word "hiring" within your zip code. (Waldman says that the number-one hashtag is #hiring, but also look at the resources list for his comprehensive list of fifty hashtags for job searches to cover all your bases.)

- **Follow other handles strategically and specifically for job search purposes.** Many universities and their career services departments are active in the job-search conversation on Twitter. You can follow them to read tweets about jobs, articles, and events relevant to your local job search in both your city and your state at large.

- **Follow industry leaders.** Stay ahead of the competition. Know the latest trends and issues for your industry by following local leaders in your area of interest.
- **Be strategic in deciding whom to follow online.** Besides finding and interacting with leaders in your professional niche, check out more global Twitter accounts such as the following.

    @JobHuntOrg: Susan P. Joyce tweets on behalf of Job-Hunt.org, posting U.S. job listings, career advice, and articles for job seekers.

    @SocialMediaJob: Dave Weinberg (@weinberg81), cofounder and CEO of Pinbooster, aggregates job listings in the social media sector.

    @CraigslistJobs: Incorporate Craigslist into your Twitter feed to receive job postings from across the United States.

    @YouTernMark: Mark Babbitt, *Huffington Post* blogger and founder of YouTern.com, tweets recruiter advice with a focus on millennials and social media.

    @BrazenCareerist: Tweets from the Brazen Careerist website include links to webinars, virtual career fairs, and recruitment events.

    @Careerealism: From the website of the same name, Careerealism shares no-nonsense blog posts about recruitment and networking.

    @DailyMuse: This feed contains career advice from The Muse, a job site where you can apply to work for companies such as Facebook, Pinterest, Spotify, and more.

    @Macs_List: You didn't think we would overlook our own Twitter account, did you? We share all kinds of actionable job search tips every day.

Mind your manners online!

It all started with a tweet. A comment on a blog led to an email exchange. You liked my Facebook update, and I thumbs-upped your Instagram photo. Five months later, I've developed an impression of you even though we've never met in person or talked on the phone. Is it a good one?

More and more we create and grow professional and personal relationships in the digital space. This happens every day as email takes the place of a phone call and Google Hangout becomes our conference room. Have you stopped to think about how you come across in your online interactions?

Email, don't text. We get it—you're a millennial; you text. But hiring managers are often Baby Boomers and Gen Xers who communicate primarily by email. Because they are hiring you, you need to use the technology they are most comfortable with. In general, email is still considered the universal language for interpersonal business communications.

Check your online etiquette when writing email. Consider how you speak to others in person. Are you bubbly and gregarious? Are you subdued and practical? You don't have to become someone you're not. But to build solid relationships in the online space, don't risk sounding rude just because you're an introvert, busy, or distracted.

- **Greetings and closings:** Trust, once broken, is not easily repaired. And trust can be lost because of a hastily written email. Make sure you use a warm greeting and close with a salutation (unless a more casual relationship has already been established). It's kind. It shows thoughtfulness and care, and it helps avoid an unintended tone of disinterest, dismissal, or rudeness.

- **Content:** When writing the body of the email, remember that tone, volume, and nonverbal cues are hard to convey digitally. Punctuation and emoticons (smiley faces) can help to convey tone and meaning, but a carefully written email will do the same. The use of emoticons in professional communication is still up for debate. "If You're Happy and You Know It, Must I Know, Too?" asks *The New York Times* in an article on business emails. It's up to you to decide whether to use a smiley face in business communications, but regardless of emoticons, stop and review what you've written one last time before hitting "Send." If the content or tone could possibly be misconstrued, consider rewriting, picking up the phone, or walking over to a desk to try to prevent an avoidable miscommunication.

- **"Reply All":** You received forty emails while you were out at lunch, of which only three are directly relevant to you and your work on a project. Enough said. Think before you hit "Reply All" and you'll save someone else the pain of an overstuffed inbox. You'll also earn their eternal gratitude.

Remember, technology is changing how we interact. Technology not only is altering the way we live our lives, but is even affecting the development of our brains. If we aren't conscious of how that affects our interactions with one another, our personal connections and relationships are likely to suffer.

Sherry Turkle, director of the MIT Initiative on Technology and Self and author of *Alone Together: Why We Expect More from Technology and Less from Each Other*, made this comment in *The Hedgehog Review* (Spring 2012): "We're moving from conversation to connection. In conversation we're present to each other in very powerful ways. Conversation is a kind of communication in which we're alive to each other, empathetic with each other, listening to each other. When we substitute Twitter or status updates on Facebook for this, we're losing something important."

With these wise words in mind, remember to make it your goal to both converse and connect in your communications with others.

Dig deeper!

For links to some of the topics covered in this chapter (including ways to optimize your use of LinkedIn, must-follow Twitter hashtags, emoticons, and business communications, among many others), go to www.macslist.org/references.

3 Networking and Conducting Informational Interviews

When you're looking for work, you need to follow this rule of the four Cs: Connect with others, Communicate your ideas, and Create Community as part of your job search. You can't do it alone! Use your connections to form relationships and get to know people who may recommend you for a job. Remember: going to networking events also shows that you're active in your community and that you're willing to go the extra mile to find the right job.

Here's why you should network.

Some people are born networkers, others acquire networking skills, and still others have networking events thrust upon them. No matter which group you're in, you need to embrace the fact that networking and informational interviews are crucial tools in your job search. They get results.

The "hidden job market" is not a myth. Some estimates put the number of unadvertised jobs as high as eighty percent. Talk to hiring managers, human resource directors, and career counselors and they'll tell you that most openings, especially for professional positions, never appear on a job board. Positions go unadvertised because employers hire people they know or who come recommended by people they trust.

Applying online isn't enough. You can't rely on just responding to the openings you see on Mac's List and other job boards. If all you do is answer job ads, you will find yourself competing with dozens or even hundreds of other applicants. Those are tough odds, no matter how qualified you may be. If you want to be in the mix, you need to make standard networking techniques such as informational interviewing, involvement in professional groups, and staying in touch with former colleagues a regular part of your professional routine.

It's a great way to hone your people skills. Networking is hard work. Like any skill, it takes time, patience, and a lot of practice. You will also experience rejection. People may ignore you at a social event, fail to answer your emails, or not return your telephone calls. Here's the good news: you have the most important asset every networker needs—a group of friends, family members, classmates, and current and past coworkers. With enough education and effort, you can master even the most advanced networking skills.

It will energize your job search. No matter how hard it may be to reach out to others while you're looking for work, talking to others is rewarding. It can also be inspiring, interesting, informative, and just plain fun. Keep reminding yourself—going out to talk to other people who share your interests and passions definitely beats staying home and binge-watching Netflix while polishing off a pint of ice cream.

You Can't Do It Alone–Help Others Help You

by **Dawn Rasmussen**, President, PathfinderCareers.com

When it comes to a job search, networking is priority number one. Yet I see a lot of people tune in and out when it comes to practicing it. "I'm too busy. I don't have time to go to this networking function." This is a huge mistake; networking is the critical lifeline.

Most people find jobs through someone they know. Gerry Crispin from CareerXroads shares a statistic: if you apply only online you have only a 2% chance of getting interviewed. But if you apply by working through someone that you know, you have about a 50% chance of getting interviewed. That stark contrast really shows how direct networking impacts your job search success. Building and nurturing relationships allows you to continue the conversation from the initial meeting point and lays the groundwork for future conversations—not only when you need to talk to your contacts, but also in situations where they may consider you for positions they have.

So what do you do if you aren't exactly the Type A networker?

There's hope.

You can grow any informal connection through continued follow-up. This doesn't mean stalking someone. Instead, try being mindful if you encounter an article or feature that might be interesting to that person, and forward a link. Wish him or her well on any announcements posted on social media. Or better yet, start setting up informational interviews.

Take the fear out of talking with unknown people by making them a known quantity, and your comfort levels will go up. That way, it is an easy conversational segue into discussing a potential job opening when they already know how you fit.

Another way to incorporate community into your job search is for you to get involved with a business or organization that interests you. I know we're all pressed for time and it's hard to carve out space for a volunteer experience, but this is a great way to get familiar with other people and similar types of jobs. Once you volunteer, you end up becoming a known quantity as you give back to that organization.

Networking and volunteering are both great ways to make yourself known. No one is going to reach out directly to you and say, "I'm going to help you throughout the rest of your career." That just doesn't happen. You have to be proactive and put yourself out there.

Work the room like a pro.

Networking is all about making connections, and your goal is to make as many meaningful contacts as possible at each event you attend. Follow these rules and you'll be the master of your own networking universe.

Prepare yourself. Set yourself up for success before you even set foot in the door.

- **Polish up your LinkedIn profile.** Upload a professional-looking headshot, update all of your information, and fill in the "Summary" section in a way that promotes who you are and what you do well. Finally, create a custom public profile URL.

- **Make business cards.** Handing out a card at an event boosts your chances of cultivating a relationship after the drinks are over. Make sure it includes your contact information and the URL to your LinkedIn profile. Create a title for yourself (graduate student, strategic communicator, social media evangelist) that helps people remember who you are or what you want to do.

- **Check the privacy settings for all of your social media platforms.** Make sure your virtual self is looking good and not unprofessional. You'll want to avoid any potential employer having the opportunity to see your photos from a rowdy Fourth of July barbecue.

- **Know your story in advance.** Have a thirty-second introduction ready that explains who you are and what your job goals are. Make eye contact and have a firm handshake ready. Wear casual business attire but include creative touches, such as an interesting accessory that may help break the ice.

- **Set goals. Know what you want to accomplish.** Have a clear idea of what you intend to gain before you arrive. Possible goals might include meeting potential employers, connecting with other job seekers for advice and support, reconnecting with current contacts and former colleagues, or identifying areas of interest or inquiry that you want to explore further.

- **Manage expectations. Begin by knowing what you want.** You don't have to walk away with a job offer for an event to be a success. Focus on building and maintaining relationships.

Don't be shy—dive right in. Once you're at the event, take a deep breath and get off to a good start by doing the following:

- **Arrive early.** The early bird catches the connections. Settle in, breathe deeply, and you'll be better company and enjoy yourself more. Don't be the person who arrives late.

- **Stand by the food or drinks.** It's easy to strike up a brief, one-on-one conversation in the buffet line or at a snack table. It's also a setting that gives you a few minutes with one person and the ability to move on if you wish.

- **Put the nametag on right.** Right-handed people instinctively put a nametag on their left side. Big mistake. To make your nametag easy to see, put it on your right—something only ten percent of us do.

- **Repeat names.** Restate the name of the person you're meeting. ("Nice to meet you, Eric. I'm Mac.") This helps you remember. Don't worry about the repetition. As Dale Carnegie said, "Names are the sweetest and most important sound in any language." (See the resource list for ten tips for remembering names.)

- **Ditch people you already know.** It's tempting to stick with people you see frequently. Instead, strike out on your own. Remember, you're there to grow your network.

- **Approach others.** See someone standing alone? He or she will be secretly relieved when you walk up, introduce yourself, and start a conversation. Not sure about joining a small group? Look for friendly body language and casual conversation, good signals they are open to talking with others.

- **Know what to say and what you want.** Come with a few stories to share that have nothing to do with work. Talk about a new movie you like, your vacation plans, or a restaurant you want to try. But be selfish, too. Is there a connection you want to make or an introduction you'd like to arrange? Have your anecdotes and asks ready before you enter the room.

- **Be memorable.** The more "important" a person is, the more people he or she will meet at a networking event. If you want the person to remember you, find a way to make a personal connection so you will stand out.

- **Ask questions and then listen to the answers.** The really smart people at a networking event don't talk and talk and talk, especially about themselves. They ask great questions. This puts others at ease. Open-ended questions work best. Ask about someone's involvement in the sponsoring organization, their connection to the host, or the distance they've traveled. You'll also hear great stories and get important insights. Knowing how to listen is one of the most valuable skills of all.

- **Be a host.** Make introductions and invite others to join a group. People will be grateful and remember your kindness.

- **Help others.** Does a conversation reveal common interests and make you think of websites, articles, or other helpful material? Offer to pass along this information. This allows you to be a resource after you return to the office and gives a legitimate reason to exchange business cards.

- **Remember: quality beats quantity.** Don't be that person who collects a stack of business cards as though they were rare baseball cards. Instead, talk to a few people with the goal of building real relationships.

- **Take notes**. After you leave an event, take a moment to jot a few facts on the back of the cards of people you've met. Reference that information in a follow-up note. Don't rely on your memory.

- **Meet on LinkedIn.** Did you have a good conversation with someone? Send a LinkedIn invitation to remain connected. Avoid the standard text and write a personal note.

- **Stay connected. Follow up.** Consider asking for—or giving—an informational interview. This could be a formal meeting in an office, a quick cup of coffee, or a lunch. If you're attending a regular lunch or event sponsored by a professional group, look for people you've met before.

Look for opportunities to network.

OK! You're convinced you need to network and you've just learned how to do it, but where do you begin? How do you find places to practice your new skills?

Tap into your existing social and professional networks. Check out professional association meetings, conferences, or other events. Whether you volunteer or simply show up, you'll make important contacts and good friends. By learning about the latest developments, you'll make yourself more valuable to your current (and future) employer. But don't stop there. Let everyone know you are looking for work—family, friends, classmates, alumni, and colleagues.

Make use of all of LinkedIn's potential. Most of us have a basic LinkedIn profile but don't take advantage of all the platform's capabilities. What you might not know is that LinkedIn is a great tool for building a network. It is easy to use—just get in there and connect with everyone you know or meet. Send them a personal note, follow up, schedule coffee with the ones you really like, keep in touch, and cultivate your network for job security, professional support, and opportunities you never even imagined.

Attend a career fair. These events can be very useful for meeting potential employers and learning about entry-level jobs and student internships. They also provide a perfect opportunity to practice and sharpen job interview skills.

Just remember to plan ahead by creating a thirty-second introduction that explains who you are and what job goals you have. Have questions ready for the people you want to meet. Avoid general queries such as, "Tell me about your company." Instead, ask about topics that demonstrate you researched the employer and are thinking about the firm's needs. Then, if you learn that an employer is hiring, ask about next steps in the process. Bring pen and paper or a smartphone to take notes and make an appointment if appropriate. Finally, make it easy for others to find you. Bring resumes and business cards so that employers can follow up with you after the event.

Go to organized networking events. Target networking events that reflect your career and professional interests. With so many events around town, it's easy to find ones that speak directly to your needs. Although nowhere near a comprehensive list, here are events and organizations that the Mac's List staff likes. (See the chapter resource list for links to these events.)

- **For professionals in general**

  GeekWire: This is a national technology news site with strong roots in the Seattle region. It coordinates its own events and meet-ups across a broad cross section of the tech community and also maintains a calender of events submitted by outside organizations and groups.

  Green Drinks International: Every month, people who work in the environmental field meet up at informal sessions known as Green Drinks. Attendees include a mix of people working in NGOs, academia, government, and business.

  National Council of Nonprofits: This is the nation's largest network of non-profit associations. It has more than 25,000 members as well as a network of state associations and nonprofit allies that cover most of the United States.

  Young Nonprofit Professionals Network: The YNPN activates emerging leaders by connecting them with resources, people, and ideas. Its more than forty chapters are located across the United States, with new start-up chapters forming frequently.

  Entrepreneurs Organization: With 157 chapter locations in forty-eight countries, EO supports entrepreneurs in all corners of the world. It sponsors global events, global universities, and conferences in the U.S. and abroad.

  Toastmasters International: With a focus on communication and leadership development, this international organization has clubs in 135 countries and most major cities. It is best known for helping members improve their speaking and communications skills to help them become better leaders.

Society for Marketing Professional Services: SMPS represents a network of marketing and business development professionals. Their site offers a variety of online and national events, while local chapters are available in most states.

Social Media Club: With hundreds of regional and international chapters, the SMC hosts global conversations related to technology and our changing society and is a good place to connect with a community of like-minded professionals.

- **For communications professionals**

American Marketing Association: The AMA has numerous local and collegiate chapters that help marketers and academics connect with other people and resources in this field.

Public Relations Society of America: This is the world's largest organization of public relations professionals. You can join a professional interest section and/or one of more than 100 local chapters.

International Association of Business Communicators: With regions and chapters throughout the world as well as the United States, this organization supports initiatives related to global communication. It hosts regional, national, and global events as well as online workshops and seminars.

American Advertising Federation: The AAF hosts a variety of events throughout the year to help further members' careers, honor their work, and engage them in all aspects of advertising.

Rotary Young Professionals: This organization celebrates the young professionals who are finding a home and a purpose as members of Rotary International. Besides this specific group, Rotary International sponsors a variety of events, learning and reference resources, and forums for the exchange of ideas.

- **For women**

Hub Dot: At Hub Dot events, attendees use colored dots instead of name tags as a way to help women start conversations and make connections in an authentic way. Hub Dot is about the cross-pollination of ideas, talent, support, and friendships.

National Association of Professional Women: This is the nation's largest networking organization for professional women. NAPW offers events in a variety of U.S. cities and has an e-chapter as well as a large number of state and local chapters.

National Association for Female Executives: One of the country's largest associations for women professionals and business owners, it provides resources through education, networking, and public advocacy.

Young Women Social Entrepreneurs: Each YWSE chapter promotes young women's leadership by providing training and development, access to resources, peer and mentor support, and networking opportunities.

- **For African-Americans**

Black EOE Journal: *The Black Employment and Entrepreneur Journal* is an African-American career and business connection whose mission is to inform, educate, employ, and provide equal opportunity. It provides diversity news, statistics on workforce diversity, recruitment and business opportunities, conferences, and event calendars.

National Black MBA Association: The organization develops partnerships that create intellectual and economic wealth in the black community through a focus on career, education, entrepreneurship, leadership, and lifestyle. It has a national conference, many state chapters, and a job board.

- **For Asian-Americans**

National Association of Asian-American Professionals: The NAAAP is a nonprofit organization that engages Asian and Pacific Islander leaders in professional development, community service, and professional networking events. The latter include a series of panels, workshops and seminars, and web-based sessions and networking.

Asian-American Professional Association: The AAPA is a nonprofit organization whose mission is to help Asian-American and minority professionals maximize their career and leadership potential. Its offerings include one-on-one mentoring, workshops and general sessions, and regular networking opportunities.

- **For Latinos and Hispanics**

    Hispanic Network **magazine:** This Latino business and employment magazine helps give Latin Americans and other minorities access to business and career opportunities. It brings promising individuals together with potential employers throughout the business community and provides diversity news and statistics, recruitment and business opportunities, conferences, and event calendars.

    The National Society of Hispanic MBAs: NSHMBA is dedicated to working with Hispanic business professionals and to increasing the number of Hispanics graduating with MBAs. It offers job opportunities, professional development, and regional networking events.

- **For the LGBTQ community**

    National Gay and Lesbian Chamber of Commerce: The NGLCC is the business voice of the LGBTQ community and is the largest global not-for-profit advocacy organization dedicated to expanding economic opportunities and advancements for LGBTQ people. It offers an events and opportunities calendar.

    Out Professional Network: Its mission is to provide the LGBTQ community with a professional network that pairs members with employers who are serious about building a diverse workforce. It provides links to resources for other diversity groups as well as to a calendar of events listed by the Professional Diversity Network.

- **For veterans**

    Veterans Business Network: This organization's goal is to develop the largest veteran-owned business database in the country. It assists veterans transitioning from military to civilian life and provides tools, connections, and a network on the web and in person at live VBN meet-ups.

    Military and Veteran Networking Forum: This annual event takes place in Washington, D.C. and is run by the Military Officers Association of America. In addition, the MOAA offers a number of career and education events throughout the year, including a virtual career fair for those who are not able to travel easily.

Request informational interviews strategically.

Now that you're putting yourself out there, you're probably making some great contacts and coming across some interesting leads to follow. Congratulations! You're ready to take the next step—asking people to give you an informational interview.

But before you start inviting people out for coffee, learn how informational interviews work and how you can use them to target specific job-hunting goals.

Start with friends and family. Turn to the people who know you best: your family and friends. Don't neglect to tell your kid sister, your neighbors, or your friends in the kickball league about your job goals and whom you want to meet.

Work your LinkedIn page. As mentioned previously, an up-to-date LinkedIn profile is vital to the success of any job search. One of the biggest advantages of staying in touch with former colleagues and fellow students on LinkedIn is that you can see their networks and where they reach. Don't be shy. Ask for an introduction if you see a connection you want to make.

Know the players. Reach out to the leaders of your occupation's professional association. Also look at published guides of leading employers such as the following.

- *The Business Journals Book of Lists*: The *Book of Lists* gives you essential information on the leading buyers, businesses, and employers in more than sixty of the U.S.'s most dynamic markets.

- *Fortune* **Magazine's 100 Best Companies to Work For**: To identify the 100 best companies to work for, each year *Fortune* partners with the Great Place to Work Institute to conduct the most extensive employee survey in corporate America.

- **The *Nonprofit Times* Best Nonprofits to Work For**: This is a national program managed by Best Companies Group, dedicated to finding and recognizing the best employers in the nonprofit industry.

- **The *Business Journals* People on the Move**: This is a *Business Journals* subscription database of thousands of people on the move across the country.

Don't forget your alma mater. Many universities have an online database of graduates, often leaders in their professions, who have offered to talk to fellow alumni about job hunting. Have you visited your school's alumni database? If not, you'll be amazed at the people who are willing to help you.

Do the following when you're ready to make contact. How do you set up the meeting? Here are guidelines to follow when asking for an informational interview, along with a sample request email. (Want to learn more about scheduling informational interviews? The JustJobs Academy has a number of resources, including email templates showing how to ask for an appointment. The Muse also has very good online resources on these topics. See chapter resource list for links.)

- **Say who sent you.** People are more likely to make time if you are introduced by someone they know, so mention your common connection.
- **Describe what you want.** Want to learn more about an unfamiliar profession? Hoping to uncover upcoming job opportunities in the field? Want introductions to other leaders? Be specific and you make it easier for others to help you.
- **Share an agenda in advance.** Explain the purpose of the meeting and how you believe the person you want to see can help. Don't leave anything to the imagination. Someone is much more likely to agree to a meeting if you tell them in advance what you want.
- **Include your resume.** No, you're not applying for a job, but your resume provides an excellent summary of your background, and those you meet will welcome this information.
- **Set time limits.** A good informational interview requires no more than fifteen to thirty minutes. Let people know this is all the time you want.
- **Follow up.** Haven't heard back? Try following "the rule of three" with any scheduling request. Make three follow-up attempts—spaced four or five business days apart—before giving up.
- **Use this as a model.** Below is an example of an email you might send when requesting an informational interview.

  SUBJECT LINE: Request for Informational Interview/Writing at Suggestion of *<contact>*

  I am writing at the suggestion of *<contact>* at *<business affiliation>*. I am exploring opportunities in *<career field>* in *<location>*. As you can see from the attached resume, I've had considerable experience creating and leading successful *<type of work>* in *<location>*.

<Contact> thought you would be good source of information about <career field> in <location>, upcoming jobs in the field, and other people I might contact. I'm hoping you might have fifteen to thirty minutes to meet with me sometime in the next few weeks.

Please let me know if this might be possible and what dates and times are most convenient for you. I look forward to hearing from you.

Best regards,
<your name>

The 20-Minute Networking Meeting

by **Nathan Perez**, Career & Job Search Coach,
Coauthor of *The 20-Minute Networking Meeting*

Often, when busy professionals receive a request for a networking meeting, time is the deciding factor as to whether or not they accept it. If you want to improve your chances of meeting an important contact, make it clear that you only want twenty minutes of his or her time.

How do you keep your meeting to twenty minutes? By having a very focused agenda and highly specific questions. Vague, broad questions lead to protracted conversations—conversations that demand too much of your contact's time and probably don't really help in your job search.

When I meet with job seekers, many of them ask questions such as: "Do you think I should find another job?" That's a very vague prompt, which requires a whole slew of clarifying questions: What exactly do you mean? Should you go find one now? Should you go find one later? A job in your same line of work, or in a whole different industry? Do you enjoy what you're doing now? These are the kind of big decisions you need to get clear about on your own before you reach out for informational interviews.

Avoid misusing the valuable time you get in informational interviews. Give your networking contact important context about your background and where you are right at this moment. Then you ask a short set of questions that are targeted and strategic. This requires you to know about your contact's background and to have some specific idea of how he or she might be able to help you. Remember, you're tapping into this person's expertise and knowledge. Always reflect on how you can best leverage this information to further inform your own job search.

Once you've prepared, the best thing you can do is listen and be actively engaged in the conversation. Staying present is really key, and that includes being aware of how much time has passed. You don't want your networking contact being distracted while checking the time.

Preparation and focus allow you to have a really powerful and informative conversation within a very short period of time. Master the art of the twenty-minute networking meeting and you'll quickly build a network that advances your job search.

Structure your interview carefully.

Your preparation shows the person you're interviewing that you've spent time in advance so that you don't waste his or hers. Follow Nathan's advice, as well as these do's and don'ts, to master the art of the informational interview.

Make sure you do this!

- **Read up in advance.** There's no excuse for not reading the company website and the LinkedIn profile of the person you're asking for help. Doing so gives you the information you need to make the most of the conversation and signals you want to use the time well.
- **Identify your goal.** Every informational interview must have a purpose. Your exact goals depend on your needs. These could include introducing yourself to leaders in your field, growing your professional network, and reconnecting with former colleagues. Be clear about what you want before you walk through the door.
- **Bring specific questions.** Come prepared with an "ask." Perhaps it's an introduction to someone at the company that interests you. Or it could be advice about how to handle challenges you face in switching careers.

Whatever the request, be specific. Email the questions if that makes you more comfortable. Don't know what to ask? Here are some ideas:

What educational background do you think is needed for the kind of work that you do?

Are there any other organizations similar to yours that I should know about and research?

Is there someone you think I should meet who might be helpful in my search for a career like yours?

What associations do you recommend I join?

Where should I volunteer in order to grow my skill set and meet people in my industry?

How can I help you?

- **Leave early for your interview.** You never know if there will be traffic, if there will be parking, or if all the buildings will be identical so that you are running around like a crazy person trying to find the right one. Give yourself enough time so that you are waiting in the lobby ten minutes early. The person you are scheduled to meet with is doing you a favor, so do not waste his or her time.

- **Be polite to everyone.** Greet everyone, smile, make eye contact, and shake hands with everyone you meet. Start your interview by saying thank you to your interviewee for taking the time to meet with you.

- **Tell your story.** Remember when we advised you to work on a quick summary of your job-hunting journey? Now's the time to tell it. It will help your listener understand what you do so that he or she can suggest contacts or remember you when a job opening comes up.

- **Ask questions and listen carefully to the answers.** Never ask for information you can read on a company website or a LinkedIn profile. Doing so says you didn't prepare. Instead, ask your questions and listen or take notes while they are answered.

- **Wind down and wrap up.** With your last five minutes, finish the interview and summarize what decisions were made and what action steps you agreed upon. Make a brief, positive goodbye and—above all—express your gratitude.

- **Ask how you can help them.** People who request informational interviews always stand out when they finish by asking what they can do for the interviewee. Don't forget that you have much to offer to others no matter what your stage of career.

- **Buy the coffee.** No one expects to be rewarded for giving an informational interview, but it's nice if the coffee is on the person making the request.

Don't make these mistakes!

- **Arrive too early.** Leave home early and try to arrive ten minutes before your interivew, but don't go to the person's office more than five minutes before the appointed time. He or she has other business. Instead, take a walk around the block or catch up on your email at a coffee shop.

- **Dress down.** Offices are much less formal these days. Business casual works most of the time. Always know the office culture, however, and avoid being too casual.

- **Forget your resume or business card.** Always offer to share your resume at the start of the meeting even when you've emailed it in advance. The person you're seeing will be grateful to review your resume again and refresh his or her memory about your background. Don't forget to exchange cards at the beginning or end of the meeting and use the information to stay in touch with your contact on LinkedIn.

- **Have no ask.** An unsuccessful meeting is one that ends without any next steps identified. Perhaps you want insights in changing careers, advice on how managers in your field hire, or introductions to new contacts. Have your list ready. The people you're meeting wouldn't see you if they didn't want to help.

- **Ask for a job.** Never ask for a job in an informational interview. You're there to network, not to apply for a position.

- **Assume unlimited time.** Your time is your most valuable asset. The same is true for the person you're meeting. You specified a certain amount of time in your request for the interview. Now stick to it. Bring the meeting to a close on schedule.

Don't drop the ball!

If you follow the steps above, you're ready to rock the informational interview. After the interview don't forget to do one last thing—follow up!

Send a thank-you note. Handwritten notes are nice. Email is just fine. Whatever the format, just do it and do so within twenty-four hours. People are busy, and while they may be willing to do informational interviews, you want to make sure that their generosity does not go unnoticed. People will notice (and remember) if you don't thank them. And while you're at it, why not include a gift card for a cup of coffee in your thank-you note? You will create terrific good will.

In the thank-you note, feel free to politely remind the interviewee of what he or she agreed to do. Examples are: "Thank you for offering to connect me with X," or "Thank you for offering to send me information about that volunteer opportunity with Y."

Connect via social media. Invite the people you meet to connect with you on LinkedIn. Look for ways to stay in touch, such as interacting with them on Twitter, Instagram, and Google+, or leaving comments on their blog or LinkedIn posts.

Stay in touch. Look for ways to remain in contact, such as forwarding relevant articles or links, sharing news about mutual contacts, or letting people know when you've found work. Don't neglect your network! Your career will be better for it.

Burn no bridges! Every city, no matter how large, is really a small town. Over the course of a career, you will keep meeting the same people. Always treat others with the same respect and courtesy you expect. You never know who may be sitting on a hiring panel or reviewing a contract proposal.

Dig deeper!

For links to some of the topics covered in this chapter (including the hidden job market, more networking tips, networking events, and informational interviewing tips, among many others), go to www.macslist.org/references.

4 Looking for Opportunities and Experience

Don't just stumble blindly through your job search! Be on the lookout for new opportunities to gain valuable work experience or skills, make formal connections with people who can give you advice and guidance, or locate specialized resources for job listings you might not otherwise encounter. If job hunting is getting you down, don't give up. Fire up your search with new experiences, professional advice, and ideas!

Be an intern.

Whether you are a recent college grad looking for your first job or someone looking to change careers, you need to get some pertinent job experience under your belt. The good news is that opportunities exist all around you—just keep your eyes open and find ways to take advantage of them.

Internships are a great way to boost your resume and ease your transition into the workforce. Whether your internship is paid or offered through an academic program, make sure that it is a good opportunity for you to acquire the skills and information you need for your chosen field. Here are some tips for maximizing the value of your internship. (*The Huffington Post* and Career Services at Princeton University also have good advice on making the most of internships. See resource list for links.)

Don't let the hierarchy scare you. It can be nerve-racking working around successful people, but don't be afraid of them. Just because someone is a "higher-up" doesn't mean that he or she won't give you the time of day. Always recognize that people are busy and their time is limited. Use your new colleagues as a resource to help you learn more about the industry or how to start planning your next step. Your coworkers are just people when you strip away the job title.

Be efficient. Look for ways to do your repetitive assignments as quickly as possible. For instance, instead of sharing documents through Dropbox, set up a live document on Google Docs. Before implementing any new method, ask for approval. Even if your bosses say no, they will appreciate your initiative.

Make deadlines. In high school, deadlines were forgiving. In college, they were firmer. In the real world, people demand that work be done on time. When you are late, you are likely messing with someone's bottom line, and most people generally don't enjoy that—at all.

Ask for new projects. If you are completing your work in a timely manner, talk to your supervisor about taking on an extra project. Perhaps you are interested in working with a particular client or you want to shadow one of your firm's staff for a day.

Ask questions. Everyone fears sounding foolish in front of an office of smart people. In some cases it may be bad not to know, but it's always worse not to ask the question. Besides, learning more was the impetus for taking an internship in the first place, right?

Switch up your routine. Vary your media intake every day. Read a different newspaper or book, watch a different news program, or rent an old movie that made a cultural impact a few decades ago. Do anything to learn something new so that you can relate to different perspectives.

Make connections. By the middle of an internship, you have proven that you are intelligent and hardworking. Now is the time to begin developing relationships with your office colleagues. Make an effort to talk with everyone in your office and connect on LinkedIn. Each person at your company is an ideal candidate for an informational interview.

Stay on top of current trends. Be well-rounded in your cultural references. Nothing is worse than a room full of people understanding a reference and you're standing in the corner scratching your head in bewilderment. Try to buff up your knowledge of popular culture—not just current, but over the last couple of decades. It never hurts to be well-rounded.

That said, be yourself. In a job climate where culture fit has become the X factor in a hiring decision, it pays not to be a drone. Indeed, there is nothing wrong with sticking out for being a little different. Better to enjoy your surroundings than to try to keep up a façade for your whole career.

Then again. . . don't be your harshest critic. It's easy to obsess over what we think of as a wrong decision. Strive to do the best you can, but know that you are human and mistakes are inevitable. Take your internship seriously, but don't be too hard on yourself if something goes wrong. Apologize, take responsibility for your mistake, and use it as a learning experience.

There's No Place for Fire Dancing During Your Internship
(and Other Tips for Being a Great Intern)

by **Jennie Day-Burget**, Communications Officer and Strategist at the Robert Wood Johnson Foundation

I've supervised many interns over the course of my career. While their backgrounds, hairstyles, and majors have varied, they all had one thing in common—limited experience in a professional environment. I don't fault them for this—most have been young, bright, and aspiring professionals who haven't had much opportunity to get professional experience yet—and that's where I can help.

Here are my tips for new interns:

Believe in yourself because I believe in you. I didn't hire you just to hire someone. I hired you because I believe you can do a job for me. Don't shy away from assignments because you worry you can't do them. You can, or you wouldn't have gotten the internship.

Check your email! We don't assign email addresses as a matter of ritual—we assign them because that's how we talk to you. There is an expectation in the business world that if I email you, you'll email me back with the information I seek in a timely fashion.

Dress for the job. We're pretty business casual around here, but by any definition of "business casual," furry winter boots and zip-up hoodies are not appropriate. Excessive cleavage makes people feel awkward, and too much perfume might kill us all. Ripped concert t-shirts really don't inspire me to think of you as someone I can turn to with a pressing request. Shorts? If I'd see it at a cabana, I probably shouldn't see it in the office.

Replace casual vernacular with professional vernacular. You're no longer conversing with your peers; you're conversing with business professionals. Adjust your language accordingly. Replace "Hey Jennie, there's a guy up front here to see you" with "Jennie, there's a gentleman up here asking for you." See the difference? By using professional language, you've proven yourself a professional and also made our office look professional. And I will like you for that.

Your success (or failure) will follow you well beyond your internship. Come in smelling like you partied your pants off at the local club's fire dancer show last night? Leave the party at the party. There's just no place for fire dancing on our (current) client roster. And workplace booze events like this will follow you. . . I promise.

Use your inside voice. I know, I know. It sounds like I'm talking to a third grader, but seriously, USE YOUR INSIDE VOICE! It's hard to concentrate when the interns parked outside of your office are recounting last weekend's kegger. I don't want to hear about it, so save that conversation for the bus.

Volunteer.

As part of your job search you should always look for opportunities to connect with like-minded people. One way to accomplish this is by volunteering. Doing so opens doors and will give you new ideas as well as concrete experience and skills. Here are some reasons that volunteering as part of your job hunt is time well spent:

It expands your network. Volunteering can open many doors to opportunities you may never have thought of and allow you to meet people outside your comfort zone. This may be just the ticket to learning about that quiet startup or a cutting-edge master's program. New connections might even steer you down a path to a great fellowship or consulting gig, exposing you to ideas and opportunities that you never even knew existed.

It boosts your morale. It's no secret that giving to the world around us makes us feel good. The job search can be hard. Volunteer your time and improve your perspective. It might just give you the boost of energy you needed to get through the week.

It bespeaks your passions. You say that caring for the environment is your passion? Employers look to your resume as proof that your actions really do align with your beliefs. They want to see that you donate your spare time to the cause you care about and that you are committed to your ideals. Volunteer positions on your resume show that you are a well-rounded individual eager to make a difference.

It lets you test out a career or new sector. Thinking of leaving your job in communications to become a midwife? Volunteer in a hospital or women's clinic before you take the plunge! You may save yourself countless hours in the classroom and lost money if you experience the industry first as a volunteer.

It lets you practice your skills or learn new ones. Are you a master at digital strategy? Volunteer your expertise with a nonprofit organization and you can build your resume and references. Thinking of quitting your day job to become a writer? Offer to create press releases or be a contributing blogger for your favorite nonprofit. You'll gain valuable experience and insight into the field.

It fills gaps in your resume. Employers generally don't like to see prolonged time gaps in your resume. Use volunteer experiences to answer the question, "What were you doing between jobs?"

To get started, check out places such as Volunteer.gov and Volunteer Match to identify organizations where you can volunteer in your area. (See chapter resource list for links.)

Try summer (or other temporary) employment.

Having a temporary summer job gives you valuable and transferable skills without making a long-term commitment to a particular profession. Summer jobs allow workers to explore the working world and learn something unique in the process.

The benefits don't apply only to students. Businesses also benefit from creating summer jobs. Summer workers offer a cost-effective way to increase an organization's productivity and also give staff members an opportunity to gain supervisory experience.

Hello College Students, I'm Talking to You!

by **Gabrielle Nygaard**, Fulbright Scholar and Former Prichard Communications Intern

The question every college senior dreads but can't avoid: "What are you going to do after graduation?" Don't despair—I have two answers for you!

Don't wait until you graduate to take action. Venture out of the bubble that insulates life at every university and into the real world now. Put yourself out there. Invest in some time off campus. Activities and accomplishments outside of your institution will serve you well for many reasons. Not only will "real world" experience hone your practical skills and provide professional connections, but it will also enhance your resume.

Employers want to see diverse experience and that you have what it takes to succeed in a professional field outside student employment, student programs, and other school-sponsored endeavors. Try an internship or volunteer position off campus. Classwork can be a good way to display your skills, but published or paid work samples will make your portfolio shine. As my friend—a recent graduate who snagged a desirable marketing job—forewarned me, outside of the school setting there are no course syllabi, assignment rubrics, and due dates to guide our work. The sooner we experience and adapt to the flow of "real" work, the better.

Consider the benefits of a bridge year. Traveling, interning, volunteering, or otherwise wandering the world will help you learn about yourself. Cultural and service experiences are the classic setups for stepping out of your comfort zone. A key to finding your career niche is to know thyself. By expanding your horizon you can explore and challenge yourself. Whether domestic or abroad, a bridge year can expose you to new ways of thinking and vast opportunities.

A bridge year is also a chance to identify and hone your personal strengths, as well as try your hand at developing new skills. What you find about your likes, dislikes, and abilities may reinvigorate or realign your career goals—and the knowledge you gain can help you reach them. By getting out of your normal sphere, you'll make all kinds of connections and new allies, both personal and professional. Not only will the experience shape you as a person, it will add something special to help yours stand out in a sea of resumes.

Find a mentor.

Let's face it: sometimes we all need a little push to help set us back on track or to help us recognize opportunities we may have missed. Finding a mentor and then setting up monthly meetings can help you reevaluate your goals and keep you from losing hope. It's also a great opportunity to receive constructive criticism from a professional in your field.

Here are three reasons it is important to have a mentor and three tips for identifying a mentor in your network:

Why do I need a mentor?

- **Professional development:** A mentor can help you identify your long-term goals and the strategies to help you achieve them. Each time you meet, you can discuss progress and obstacles and set goals for the future.

- **Professional support:** Mentors can keep you going and point out opportunities you may have missed. They can also help you with your resume and lead you to key resources.

- **Creative thinking:** Brainstorming with someone who isn't mired in your specific challenges often produces great ideas. Struggling with how to find internships or volunteer opportunities? Check in with your mentor to identify new areas to research.

How do I find a mentor?

- **Identify someone.** Look at your network of people. Whom do you admire the most and why? Does this person do something well that you'd like to learn about? Is he or she an expert in an area where you are looking to grow? Many professional organizations also offer mentorship programs and networks. (Check the list of professional organizations in Chapter 3 as well as the job resources on pages 41-44.)

- **Know your strengths and weaknesses.** In identifying a mentor, understand your own needs. Are you exploring work in new sectors? Starting your own business? Looking for ways to grow professionally? Find a person who has been there and can help you navigate the challenges.

- **Ask.** Many people agree to be a mentor purely for the sense of satisfaction in paying it forward. Start by simply asking for advice on one action or problem and then continue the relationship by showing how they can help you.

Know where to find local job listings.

When looking for work, you can't rely on one source alone to learn about publicly advertised jobs. You need to diversify. Local job search boards are a terrific way to find openings that may never appear on the big national job sites. (And oh hey, by the way, did we mention that Mac's List is Portland's top source for jobs in the city and throughout Oregon at large? We did? OK, let's move on then...)

Here are some of the specialized job boards, lists, and blogs that we find particularly helpful. (See links to these in the chapter resource list.)

Public relations and communications

- **Public Relations Society of America:** The PRSA Jobcenter allows you to search openings by job function, industry, organizational setting, job type, and state.

- **International Association of Business Communicators:** At the IABC Job Centre you can search listings using a variety of filters, including location.

- **MediaBistro:** Here you can refine your search by media category, including PR & Communications, as well as job titles, keywords, companies, and location.

- **PR Crossing:** This site advertises itself as the largest collection of PR jobs anywhere and offers a wide variety of search filters.

Fundraising and development

- **Association of Fundraising Professionals:** AFP's Career Center allows you to create an account you can use to keep track of your search and save openings you are interested in.

- **Philanthropy News Digest:** PND's job board provides listings of current full-time job openings at tax-exempt organizations.

- **Supporting Fundraising:** This is an aggregator of many different job boards in the fundraising and advancement communities.

"Green" jobs

- **EcoEmploy:** Since 1998, David Brierley has published EcoEmploy.com, which features jobs from all fifty states. It lists environmental jobs as well as government jobs and includes other references related to job searching (resume tips, career information, etc.).

- **Leonard Adler's Green Jobs Network:** This site empowers people seeking careers in sustainability and environmental responsibility to find jobs, career resources, and build their professional network.
- **Green Collar Blog:** This is an aggregate listing of job boards that focus on social or environmental responsibility.
- **Greenjobsearch.org:** You can browse jobs and career resources by city on this job board for sustainability and environmental positions.
- **Greenbiz:** This job board lists job roles with a focus on green energy, green business, and green project management.

Film and television industry

- **Media Match:** This site lists employment opportunities and news in the areas of film, TV, music, and gaming. You can search the listings by job type, location, and keyword.
- **Mandy's Jobs in Film and TV:** This is a comprehensive guide to independent film and TV production resources. The site maintains a detailed directory of 100,000+ production companies, filmmakers, production crews, and equipment.
- **FTP Film and TV Pro:** This is a networking site for film and TV industry professionals. Its job list is searchable by job type and state.
- **Production Hub:** This global network of local crew and vendors has a job board with listings for jobs in film, television, video, and digital media production.
- **Staff Me Up:** This job board offers lists of production jobs in the film, TV, digital, media, and entertainment industries.

Nonprofit and government sectors

- **The National Council of Nonprofits:** This network of state nonprofit associations maintains a job board for jobs in the nonprofit sector. You can search by location or category.
- **The NonProfit Times:** Career Match is the name of the job board run by this nonprofit publication. Its career center offers job listings and resources. You can also create a profile and post your resume.
- **Idealist:** This is probably the country's largest aggregator of jobs in the nonprofit sector.

- **Work for Good:** This job board helps job seekers who are looking for work with mission-oriented organizations. Its list offers a variety of search filters, including location, job function, salary range, willingness to travel, experience level, and more.

- **USA Jobs:** This is the federal government's official employment website. You can create an account that contains your profile and resume and then use it to apply for various jobs.

- **GovernmentJobs:** This website allows you to search government job listings by type, job title, category, and location. You can also apply for these jobs online and check your application status after it is submitted.

Business and Finance

- **Association for Financial Professionals:** AFP is the professional society that represents financial executives around the world. Their job board contains several thousand up-to-date jobs.

- **eFinancial Careers:** This board includes over 10,000 jobs in finance, banking, accounting, and insurance.

- **Financial Job Bank:** Part of the Beyond.com network, Financial Job Bank specializes in accounting and finance jobs, from entry-level vacancies to more advanced positions.

- **Sales Gravy:** This is a go-to resource for anyone involved in the sales industry.

Healthcare

- **Health eCareers:** This board connects qualified healthcare professionals—from physicians and nurse practitioners to non-clinical staff—with medical providers looking for top talent.

- *New England Journal of Medicine's* **Career Center:** Managed by one of the leading academic medical journals, this site offers a wide array of opportunities for doctors around the country.

- **PracticeLink:** This is one of the oldest, largest, and most respected physician employment search engines.

- **Nursing Jobs:** This site is great for RNs, LPNs, and LVNs looking for permanent, per diem, and travel nursing opportunities.

- **AlliedHealthCareers:** This job board is for health care professions outside of the nursing, medicine, and pharmacy specialties.

Technology

- **Albert's List:** This site is an online community for job seekers looking for work in the technology sector. It's a great way to get connected with recruiters and find job referrals.
- **AngelList:** This site is great for finding jobs at start-up tech companies, although most gigs are clustered in Silicon Valley, New York, LA, and Boston.
- **Job Fusion:** This is an aggregator of jobs posted on multiple platforms. The search functionality allows you to look for jobs based on specific skills and company type.
- **Stack Overflow:** A go-to online forum for programmers, their job site offers a wide array of work opportunities for anyone with software development skills.
- **We Work Remotely:** This site list tech jobs that are available, regardless of your physical location.

Additional sources for temporary employment, internships, and volunteer opportunities

For internships, check out InternMatch.com, a national website based in San Francisco that features many paid summer jobs and internships. In addition, the National Education Association partners with institutions of higher education and other organizations to identify intern candidates.

Besides the volunteer resources mentioned earlier in this chapter, you can also discover volunteer positions at the United Way's national website.

Dig deeper!

For links to some of the topics covered in this chapter (including places to find mentors, volunteer toolkits, and sources for job listings, among many others), go to www.macslist.org/references.

5 Applying for a Job

Let's face it—the world is full of smart, creative, hardworking, and talented people (just like you!). But because of that, you need to work even harder to catch the eye of a potential employer. How do you make your job application stand out in a crowd? Let us be your guide along the route traveled by all the savvy job seekers who've come before you.

Line up your references.

Before you start applying for jobs, make sure you've got your references primed and ready in advance. Handing a potential employer your references seems like a simple step in the application process, but it can be a very important key to getting an offer. A great reference can be your ticket to that new job, while a bad one can unwind all of your hard work. Here's what you need to do before you give a potential employer your references.

Only put down great references. Don't list someone as a reference if he or she might only give you an average review. You need an advocate on your side, someone who will unequivocally support your future employment. If you're unsure, take that person off your reference list today or follow up beforehand to assure a stellar recommendation.

Make it easy. Get the updated contact information for your references and include the name, company, title, email address, and phone number. Also, note your relationship to this person—is he or she a past supervisor, employee, professor, or peer? Also be sure to note how long you have known each reference.

Give your references a heads up. To be a savvy job seeker, contact your references to let them know that they might receive a phone call or email from your potential employer. This gives your reference time to prepare and makes sure that he or she is ready to communicate and isn't caught off guard. If you land an interview, reconnect afterwards to share what particular skills the employer is looking for in the ideal candidate.

Know how to finesse a bad reference. Worried about your current boss giving you a bad review? Vicki Lind, a career counselor and marketing coach, suggests avoiding the negative, if possible, by writing "Please do not contact" when providing the name of your current supervisor. Potential employers will assume it is because you don't want that person to know you are looking for work. If you can't avoid a negative reference, consider requesting more time by adding "Prefer to discuss in person." If you are drawn into a discussion about that reference, show integrity and honesty. Describe the conflict yourself without criticizing your ex-employer. Pivot in a way that allows you to bring the focus back to your strengths, not your weaknesses.

Ace your application.

Sometimes landing a new job is a matter of luck. You don't know who might tell you about an unadvertised opening or how you will hit it off with a potential employer in an interview. What you can control is how you apply for a job. Here are some general do's and don'ts for acing the job application process.

Do. . .

- **Target your applications.** The best cover letters and resumes frame your skills and qualifications around the employer's particular needs. Whether you're applying for a government job or to a private business, use keywords from the position description; both sectors rely on automated tracking systems to screen applications. Yes, it takes more time to do this, but it will put you ahead of those who email a generic set of application materials.
- **Include a cover letter.** A good cover letter, written specifically for the job you want, always stands out. Not sending a cover letter is a lost opportunity and signals a lack of interest on your part.
- **Show that you have the education and experience to make the employer's life easier.** For example, did you win an award for a social media campaign you produced? Tell an employer how that experience has prepared you to tackle the company's social media strategy.
- **Demonstrate that you did your research.** Don't email an application if you haven't looked at the hiring company's or the organization's website and you don't know what they do.

- **Share your enthusiasm.** Nothing wins over potential employers like someone who shows excitement when talking about the job description. Don't just stop there. Say how excited you are to try something new!

Don't . . .

- **Lie or misrepresent yourself.** Avoid fiction on your resume, be it hyperbole or straight-up fabrication. It will catch up to you in the end. Find the most effective way to present your qualifications and skills, but make sure everything is solidly grounded in fact.
- **Make a typo.** Typographical errors are the fastest way to move your resume to the rejection pile. Catch typos—and mistakes in spelling, punctuation, and grammar—by reading your application aloud, a favorite tactic of famed writing coach William Zinsser. The ear is your best editor.
- **Ignore minimum qualifications.** No employer expects you to have every skill in a position announcement, but you need to meet the minimum qualifications, such as a college degree. Someone fresh out of college, for example, shouldn't apply for a job that asks for ten years of professional experience.
- **Talk only about yourself.** Employers want to know how you can solve their problems. Yes, express your enthusiasm for the opportunity, but use your cover letter and an interview to show what you can do for a company and how you can make your new supervisor's life easier.
- **Gimmick up.** Avoid adding scent to your resume unless you're Reese Witherspoon in *Legally Blonde*. Don't tell jokes, make puns, or use sarcasm in a cover letter. Ditch the colored stationery and keep the design of your resume clear and simple.
- **Be too humble.** Humility is a good quality and shows discipline, but you have bragging rights when it comes to getting a job. Don't be afraid to let your hard work shine, be confident, and tell employers why you are the one who can make their life easier. Find the balance and wow them!

Three Secrets to Success with Human Resources

by **Melissa Anzman**, CEO, Launch Your Job

There is a science to working with a Human Resources department. Of course, there are some variations depending on the company and its size, but some general rules apply to most HR departments. Here are three ways you can work with them to get your foot in the door and move along in the hiring process.

1. Personal value proposition. HR gets a ton of resumes, with a lot of qualified candidates for every open job. It's up to you to market and showcase yourself for them. Make it very easy for them to say yes to you. Know what value you bring to the table and tell them that early, often, and repeatedly during the process.

Unless you already have a connection within the HR department, your resume is the first—and perhaps only—vehicle you have to showcase your value. Don't include a bullet point list of your skills. That doesn't help HR. They want to see results-oriented, metric-driven, quantifiable data on your resume. It is absolutely imperative that you "show, don't tell" your abilities.

Make sure your online presence reflects the abilities, accomplishments, and competencies in your resume. If HR is interested in you, they will Google your name. So make sure there's enough online material to back up your value proposition. Update your LinkedIn profile to ensure it's up to date. And if you've positioned yourself as a subject matter expert, there needs to be some proof of this on the internet.

2. Networking and outreach. The next step is one that I personally dreaded for a long time. It's all about networking and outreach. You're trying to get this HR person interested enough in you that they'll want to meet in person. Don't just follow up by sending an email to careers@entercompanyname.com. Spend ten minutes or so on LinkedIn and Google to find the email address of the right person in HR. (You may sometimes have to guess. . . that's OK!) Send him or her a note and express your interest. Show your value proposition in your email, but keep it short.

3. **Understanding your audience.** When talking with HR, make sure you know their role in the hiring process. Their expertise is to recruit, not to know all the technical aspects of your prospective role. They are looking at culture fit and your personality, trying to understand if you have the basic skills for the job. They are not interested in knowing nitty-gritty details that make no sense to anybody outside your industry or your position. As soon as you start talking to that person about things that make no sense to them, you've lost your connection.

So while you want to look informed and skilled, make sure your interactions with HR are more high level in nature. Be professional, be direct, and be polite. Remember that once you have HR on your side, you have a strong advocate pushing for you to be hired.

Create a great resume. (Or two. Or three. . .) It's easy to get stuck on tactical questions when you create your resume and agonize about whether to include an objective statement, add college graduation dates, or mention hobbies. No matter what tactics you use, the applications of successful candidates share some common characteristics. Here are ideas and suggestions to keep in mind when you are creating or updating your resume.

- **Keep your audience in mind.** The person reading your resume wants to know how you can help him or her. According to Dawn Rasmussen, chief resume writer and president of Pathfinder Writing and Career Services, providing a list of accomplishments is one thing, but demonstrating how those accomplishments contributed value to your previous employers is key. How did you help your coworkers achieve their goals? How much time or money did you save them? Try to assign quantifiable (i.e., numeric) results to each accomplishment you list.

- **Keep it simple.** Good resumes adopt plain and simple design principles. Use classic fonts like Helvetica or Times New Roman for body copy, and apply bold and italic with restraint. Boxes, screens, and other flashy tricks can distract readers and confuse automated scanners. Keep it simple and easy to read.

- **Avoid age bias.** Laura Schlafly, founder of Life Choices with Laura, specializes in working with midlife professionals. She suggests avoiding age discrimination by deleting the following items.
  - An objective statement: Skip it and instead state how you'll help solve problems.

- "References Available Upon Request": Omit this completely.
- Complete chronological resume: Don't list every job you've had, along with your title and duties. Instead, show relevant skills, work ethic, leadership, and problem-solving abilities.
- Old email domains: Get rid of AOL, EarthLink, Teleport, and other once-popular email address domains introduced in the 1990s that reveal your age.

- **Update your resume for every job**. Thanks to the Internet, a job opening today can attract hundreds of applications. To stand out, you need to revise your resume to match your accomplishments and skills for every job posting. Another reason to do this, as we mentioned above, is that many companies use tracking systems to scan resumes for keywords. Applications missing the relevant phrases never make it to human reviewers. So don't forget to include as many keywords as possible.

- **Get professional help if you need it**. Have you had multiple interviews and no job offers? How about over ten years of work experience you're trying to cram into a one-page resume? Maybe it's time to consult a professional. Hiring a career-service provider is a personal decision, and while it may not be necessary for everyone, it can help when you feel stuck.

Resume writers, career coaches, career-management coaches, and life coaches all charge a fee for their services but can be a lifesaver for someone who needs support, guidance, or resume-writing assistance. So how do you find someone who is right for you? Talk to at least three different people to see who is the best fit, then follow up by checking them out online. Find out how much they charge, but don't make your decision based on price alone. Look for someone you connect with and then go with your gut. Think of it as an investment. Don't be discouraged by the fees that writers and coaches charge, because in the end you'll get what you pay for.

Create an even greater cover letter. Many job candidates often think of their cover letter as a last-minute item. Yet the letter that accompanies your resume has a very specific purpose. It demonstrates your knowledge of the organization and the position you are applying for. It is also a litmus test of your overall writing and communication skills.

A cover letter is a great vehicle for grabbing attention and holding it. Here are some tips for making the most of this opportunity when you apply for your next job.

- **Read up.** Research the company's or organization's goals, mission, and history. Find out whether it has been in the news recently and, if so, why. Learn as much as you can about its background and current needs. Don't forget to include references to that information, so that the reader knows you have done your homework.

- **Get personal.** If possible, find out the name of the decision maker and then address the cover letter directly to that person. Use a last name unless you have been introduced or referred by someone. In matters of etiquette, it's always better to err on the side of caution!

- **Be original.** Open with some kind of attention-grabbing statement or question that makes the reader want to learn more about you and your background.

- **Explain how you can solve problems.** Study the hiring company's social media accounts, read its blog posts, and show how your experience and skills will be an asset to the company. Explain your ideas here (and later on, in your interview).

- **Have a headline.** Susan Rich, founder of RichWriting, says a cover letter should focus on one main headline and two to three supporting statements about who you are and what problems you can solve.

- **Keep it active.** Stick to the point and use the active voice. When possible, use language from the company's or organization's website or social media accounts. Try to imitate the style of its communications as much as possible.

- **Avoid repetition and trite language.** Don't summarize your resume, and don't fall back on formulaic expressions that contribute little to your message. Stay away from slang, jargon, or clichés. Keep things straightforward, direct, and simple.

- **Follow the rule of three for a short but dynamic cover letter.** Have three key points and three sentences per paragraph. If your letter is longer than a page, you may be over-sharing or rambling.

- **Ask for the interview.** Always conclude with an ask. Request an interview and then follow up in a timely manner by phone or email.

Remember, the people who read your cover letters have already seen thousands of cover letters in their lifetimes! You want to make them interested in learning more about you and your application, not bore them to tears or alienate them altogether.

Your Generic Cover Letter, as Experienced by a Hiring Manager

by **Jenny Foss**, Owner, JobJenny.com

To Whom It May Concern:

I am applying for your open job with this generic, form-looking cover letter.

It is in 12-point Times Roman, with perfect one-inch margins around all sides.

I should probably warn you in advance that this letter will paralyze you with boredom and tell you virtually nothing new about me. In fact, I'm going to reiterate exact phrases from my resume, just in case you missed them over there.

I'm also going to pad this thing generously with a bunch of empty, overused clichés, including "detail oriented," "outside-the-box" and "proven track record." I may even throw in the term "very unique" because what's better than being unique? You got that right—being VERY unique. Which is me. (I'm sure you can already tell this from the letter, right?)

I'm guessing you're going to know in an instant that I am currently wallpapering the universe with this same letter (cut and paste is such a magical thing, don't you think?). But I'm very, very busy, so this is the only practical way someone so very unique (and busy) as I can go about this job search thing.

I'm sure you'll understand.

Throughout this letter, I will also use a terse, robotic tone that will give you zero indication of my personality. It's my fun little way of challenging you to figure out on your own if I'm going to fit in around the place once you hire me, which I'm sure you will.

Oh yes, before I go further, let me tell you what I want in my next job. In fact, let me outline in detail what I want throughout my career, just so you know that I expect frequent accolades, raises, and promotions should I join your organization.

You are hanging on the edge of your seat wondering how you can meet my needs, yes?

Finally, I will go off on a strange, irrelevant tangent that leaves you wondering why I even dropped those two sentences into this letter. This is my attempt at standing out.

Thank you, sir, for your consideration. I look forward to meeting you soon.

Sincerely,

Your Next Big Thing

Follow the rules of the application process and form. Whether you are working with human resources or applying for a government job, you may need to fill out a standardized form. Pay close attention to exactly what that document requires and the deadlines involved. You won't get past the first step of the hiring process if you make a rookie error or miss a deadline early on in the hiring process. Proofread your work carefully or, even better, ask a friend to do a quick review of your work. Do not, under any circumstances, ask for more time or miss the due date!

Insider Tips for Landing a Government Job

by **Kirsten Wyatt**, Cofounder, Engaging Local Government Leaders

A career in the public sector can be incredibly rewarding—and there's no better way to serve the needs of others, your community, and your nation than a job with government. Unfortunately, government hiring processes—from the local level, all the way up to the federal government—are often complicated and outright byzantine. All this makes it very difficult for job seekers to get a foothold in the public sector.

I've spent most of my career in public service and been involved in many hiring committees. Here's my advice for anyone looking to get a job in government.

First, understand the form of government where you're applying. Every government entity has its own process, standards, requirements, and hierarchies. You need to make sure you're following the right process within each institution. For example, don't approach your mayor for a job; in most cases, elected officials have little influence over the hiring process. Instead, get to know the city manager and other professional staff who run day-to-day operations.

This leads to my second recommendation: network. If you've identified an agency or office where you'd like to work, look for connections you may have within (and around) that entity. Use your network to get an inside scoop on the job. Then seek out the hiring manager and ask for a conversation to learn more. In my experience, most government workers—at least at the local level—are open to these conversations.

That being said, no amount of networking will allow you to skip formal application review and vetting. To succeed, you still need to respect the established process. Government hiring processes have become more sophisticated, and we've started using tools like NEOGOV, a standardized application aggregator. That means it's becoming more likely that you'll see an application screening process that looks for keywords from the job description. Make sure that you're tailoring your skills and abilities to the job requirements and the terminology used in the job description.

I also encourage you to join Emerging Local Government Leaders (ELGL). We're an affordable local government professional association that will allow you to build your network, learn about topics in local government, and continue your professional education.

Create a professional portfolio.

If your work lends itself to a "show-and-tell" presentation, consider creating a professional portfolio. Even if at first glance it doesn't seem like your experience is all that visual, you may still be able to come up with ways to illustrate what you do. Adding images to your career accomplishments creates an additional layer of information and appeal for potential employers.

- **Tell your story.** Tell your career story in a way that is concise, on point, and engaging. A portfolio is a visual aid to help you tell your story—not a substitute. Pointing to examples of your work is great, but you must practice your pitch so that you don't ramble or rely too heavily on the portfolio to drive the conversation.

- **As in your cover letter and resume, point to the bottom line.** Potential employers always want to know how you can solve their problems. So it is important, even in a portfolio, to show that. Did you implement a social media strategy for a nonprofit? Quantify your success and highlight in your portfolio piece and in your presentation how your projects helped achieve company objectives. Did your social media strategy grow awareness or raise money? Showcase the outcome in a way that demonstrates your value as an intern or an employee.

- **Make an e-portfolio (in addition to a physical one).** Don't simply create the traditional portfolio in print form; work up an online e-portfolio so that potential employers can just click on something. There are many sites where you can get help, such as Electronic Portfolios. (See link in chapter resource list.)

Understand how recruiters work.

At some point during your career, you will probably get a call or an email from a recruiter or headhunter. Ironically, you may tend to hear from them frequently when you are not looking for work, yet find you can't catch their attention at all when you're in the middle of a job search.

What you need to know about recruiters is that they work directly for clients who are paying them to find qualified candidates. They are not in the business of serving as a career coach or counselor. Yet sometimes, when the moon is right and the planets are in the correct alignment, their needs may line up with your needs and you may suddenly find yourself in a mutually beneficial situation.

Arnie Fertig, head coach at JobHunterCoach, interviewed Brett Harwood of Portland's G4recruiters for the Mac's List blog. In the interview, Brett shared his suggestions for job seekers who want to attract the attention of head-hunters in their field.

- **Be proactive.** Don't rely on emails or online resume submissions alone. If you want recruiters to help you, help them by providing a list of the top twenty companies where you'd like to work and explain why.

- **Put yourself on YouTube.** Make a two-minute video of yourself. Post it on YouTube, and provide a link to it at the bottom of your resume. By doing so, you can communicate why you should be taken seriously, and present your accomplishments, skills, and value. When recruiters and hiring managers view your video, they will have the ability to judge how you present yourself: your voice, enthusiasm, body language, and overall personality.

- **Pay for the premium account on LinkedIn.** Once you do, you'll be able to see the full list of who has looked at your profile. More importantly, recruiters outside your network will be able to contact you. That's in addition to the other benefits offered by the premium membership.

- **Pick up the phone.** Recruiters get tons of unsolicited resumes each week, most of which are ignored. But if you take the initiative and give them a call you'll have an easier time making a connection. The bottom line: regardless of today's technologies, nothing beats the tried-and-true method of picking up the phone and making human-to-human contact. The direct approach is also a great way to demonstrate your interest and hunger to succeed.

Dig deeper!

For links to some of the topics covered in this chapter (including cover letter and resume tips, government jobs, electronic portfolios, local recruiters, and *Legally Blonde* and scented resumes, among many others), go to www.macslist.org/references.

Interviewing and Self Marketing

When it comes to job interviews, it's just like your mother told you—it never hurts to be polite. Focusing on the interviewer's time, needs, and perspective gives you an edge on your competitors while showing that you are both a courteous and strategic career professional. Want to nail your next job interview? Here's what to do before, during, and after that important meeting or phone call.

Prepare yourself for the interview.

Do your homework ahead of time in order to set yourself up for a successful interview.

Find out about the person(s) you are meeting. It's acceptable to ask who will interview you. Study the interviewers' biographies and blogs, and visit their social media accounts. Look for shared interests and common connections. People want to work with people they know or who are known to people they trust, so keep an eye out for a mutual friend or colleague who can serve as a reference. Building this kind of rapport makes a manager more comfortable with you.

Understand what the employer needs. Don't forget to consider the hiring process from the perspective of the employer. Employers hire people to solve problems, and candidates who understand this always stand out. Talk about how you can make an employer's life easier before you discuss how a job meets your personal and professional goals. You'll be a much stronger candidate if you remember that a company has a set of problems that you may be ideally suited to solve.

Also remember that as you sit down for your job interview, one or more of the following unspoken topics are likely to be on an employer's mind:

- **Culture fit overrides expertise.** Being the smartest person in the room isn't enough to land the job. Employers put personality traits ahead of technical skills, so look for ways to show how you understand and fit into a company's culture.

- **"I needed someone two months ago!"** A hiring process can be like a home remodel project: it often takes twice as long as planned. As a result, employers may be in a hurry to make up for lost time.
- **The work is piling up.** Whether a job is a new or an old position, it exists because it meets a need. In other words, important tasks, some now perhaps urgent, aren't being completed and clients may be dissatisfied.
- **The staff is unhappy doing two jobs.** Only so much work can be postponed. In the meantime, current staff—perhaps already stretched thin— have to plug the gap, adding more pressure to hire sooner rather than later.
- **The field of candidates is small.** Yes, hundreds of people may have applied. Don't let those odds intimidate you, however. Those applicants aren't in the running anymore.

Research the company, agency, or organization. Find out whatever you can about the place where you are seeking employment. Identify the challenges it faces and prepare examples of how you have handled similar problems. Look for specific information about its products, policies, and practices so that you can ask specific and strategic questions during your interview.

Prepare and practice. Identify the key questions you think you will be asked, about both the job and your skills. Many websites have example interview questions. (See the chapter resource list for two of them.) Practice interviewing and answering questions in front of your friends or a mirror for at least twenty minutes. A mirror can help assure that you are making eye contact and not fidgeting. Or tape your rehearsal and watch the playback.

Interviewers tend to use three common themes to generate questions.

- **"Why you?"** Think about why you deserve the job over other applicants. Consider what skills you can offer and what problems you can solve.
- **"Why did you apply for this job?"** Don't simply say you need the money— think deeper about your short- and long-term career goals.
- **"Why are you interested in this company?"** Research the company and what it does. Employers want someone who is enthusiastic about the company and can bring something new.

Come with your own questions. Bring a list of questions, especially ones that focus on the employer's needs. You'll show that you are putting their concerns first while creating an opportunity to explain how you would tackle those challenges.

Dress to impress. Dress business casual or research the company to see whether a suit is necessary. Offices are much less formal these days, so business casual works most of the time. Always know the office culture, however. Avoid being too casual; always err on the side of being too formally attired.

Arrive on time, but don't arrive too early. Don't get there more than five minutes before an appointment. You don't want to add additional pressure to your interviewer's already packed schedule.

Don't forget your resume. Offer to share your resume before you begin. It's a good way to break the ice and gives the interviewer the chance to refresh his or her memory without having to be obvious about it.

Breathe! Take a few deep breaths while you are waiting. Concentrate on your breathing rather than your nerves to set your mind at ease. If you have the chance, go to the bathroom or a private space and stand for two minutes with your arms overhead and your legs apart, making your body into a large X shape. This expansive pose can cause a spike in testosterone and a drop in cortisol, which can lead to feelings of calm empowerment.

Remember that you got the interview for a reason. The hiring committee already saw something promising in you, so don't let your nerves keep you from landing your dream job!

Be Prepared! The Three Topics You Should Research Before an Interview

by **Don Raskin,** Author of *The Dirty Little Secrets of Getting Your Dream Job*

There's no doubt about it: interviews are stressful. But the more you prepare before you walk into the interview room, the better you'll perform during the conversation. The key to interview preparation is research—knowledge is power. Take the time to research these three critical topics: the company, the job, and the people with whom you are interviewing.

To learn about the company, all you need to do is go to the company's website and social media profiles, and pull out key facts about the business, the management team, the products and services, and the philosophy. You will use those facts in your interview, dropping them in as appropriate. You should also look for recent news items about the company, its competitors, and the industry at large. This makes you look smart and shows the interviewer that you did your homework and came prepared.

You also need to understand the job at hand. One of my favorite interview questions is to ask candidates to describe the job they are currently applying for. Surprisingly, that question often trips them up. So before the interview, go back to the description of the job and review the duties and responsibilities. Then, go on Indeed.com or other job sites and look at similar positions in other companies to compare the requirements and responsibilities for those jobs. If you put it all together, you will have a pretty good feel for what the job is all about.

You also need to know your interviewers. For this purpose, LinkedIn is your go-to resource. Most professionals have a LinkedIn profile where you can learn more about their work history, education, and shared connections. Don't worry about the interviewer knowing that you've viewed their profile. I actually like it when candidates check me out on LinkedIn prior to an interview. It tells me that they are doing their homework and are coming into the interview fully prepared for a good conversation.

Make the most of your interview.

Follow these tips to make a great first impression.

Know how to handle a phone interview. Employers often screen applicants with a phone interview. Not only are they making sure you're sane and reasonably intelligent, they also want to make sure both the candidate and employer are on the same page regarding location, salary, availability, and qualifications.

A phone interview can be easy to "under-think," given the informality of a phone call and the casual location in which you may be taking the call. Here are three suggestions to help you perform well during phone interviews:

- **Walk, stand up, or sit up straight in a chair.** Choose whatever pose it takes to keep you active, dynamic, and focused. Lounging, lying down, sprawling, or anything that feels relaxed and casual will come out that way in your voice.

- **Prevent interruptions.** This may sound like a no-brainer, but it's important to take care of the small things. Will outside noises disrupt you? Is your dog going to bark at the mail carrier? Is somebody going to send you a mass of texts? Small things can distract both you and the interviewer.

- **Limit computer distractions.** Keep your computer at the ready during a phone interview, providing easy access to your resume, a job description, and background on the company or interviewer. But don't let anything else happen on your computer screen. Videos, music, email, and Twitter feeds distract you, so turn them off.

Use your interview to learn about the office culture. During an in-person interview, you are there for the interviewer to meet and evaluate you and your skills. But don't forget that you are also there to evaluate your interviewer and the workplace. Use your interview to learn about the office and to take a hard look around you.

Workplace culture can vary widely. Not every office—even the trendiest of locations—is filled with young creatives who bring their pets to work. Whether you're applying at a startup firm or a traditional top-down company, it's important to learn as much as you can about a workplace's culture, both before and during a job interview. Understanding a manager's style, how staff relate to each other, and what the office environment is like helps you present well and make an informed decision about a job offer.

In addition, how a company organizes and runs a job selection process can say a great deal about its daily operations. Here are three areas to observe during the interview process that can give you insights into how a workplace functions and whether it's a good fit for you.

- **Punctuality:** Is the interviewer on time? If you are kept waiting for more than forty minutes for a job interview while the manager checks his or her phone, you might want to think twice. That kind of tardiness speaks volumes about how a person might work with employees

- **Workplace:** Are you comfortable working in a bullpen, or do you prefer a workspace of your own? Be sure to see where you will work before accepting an offer.

- **Collaborative vs. competitive:** Some people thrive in a competitive atmosphere. Others prefer a collaborative environment. Be clear about your own preference and what the potential employer offers. Need more information about office culture and the interview process? The Muse offers a list of the best questions to ask if you want to learn more about an organization's culture. (See link in the chapter resource list.)

Stick to your talking points during the interview. Remember all that prepping and self-evaluation you did before the interview? Put it in play and show your interviewer that you've done your research, you've already analyzed how your skills and experience fit the position, and you're ready to learn more. Here are three ways to keep the interview on the right track:

- **Demonstrate knowledge.** Remember, this is not just an interview but also a conversation about you as a potential employee. Show your interest in the company by discussing transitions, challenges, and successes that the organization has experienced. Doing this in a dynamic and conversational way not only signals that you've done your homework but also reflects your confidence. Phrases like "Correct me if I'm wrong, but I see that . . ." or "I may be mistaken, but in my research it appears that . . ." open the dialogue for a conversation that positions you as eager to learn and to help.

- **Point to strengths.** Maybe you're a great networker, a genius at streamlining processes, or a wonderful project manager. Whatever your skills may be, now is the time to describe how those strengths apply to this job. Don't be shy. Employers want to hire people who have put thought into their career decisions. Show them that you are eager to put your strengths and skills to work on their behalf.

- **Solve problems.** Get creative if you have to, but it is important to show that you understand an employer's needs. Don't know a company's budget or its strategic plan? Look at historical data, ask questions, and think on your feet to come up with solutions to an organization's problems.

Don't get rattled by hard questions. It's not an urban legend—hard questions do happen in job interviews. Glassdoor, an online career community and database, recently released a list of the top twenty-five oddball questions that job candidates were asked. "On a scale from one to ten, rate me as an interviewer" and "What song best describes your work ethic?" are real examples of these curveballs.

Why do they ask such hard questions? According to Samantha Zupan at Glassdoor, "Employers are looking to understand how candidates think, how they process and approach difficult brainteaser questions, and how candidates think on their feet when in a stressful situation."

If you are asked some of these kinds of questions, keep your sense of humor as well as your sense of perspective. Here are a few questions from the list and some suggestions on how to answer them:

- **"How many cows are in Canada?"** Employers aren't looking for a correct answer. Really. Who knows how many cows are in Canada? So think your way through these hard questions with creativity. Show your problem-solving skills by saying, "I would need some time to research this, but I assume there are two cows for every vegan and one cow for every vegetarian in Canada." It's a pithy answer and demonstrates a sense of humor as well.

- **"What kitchen utensil would you be?"** Coming up with an answer to an absurd question like this shows how you can think on your feet and act with courage. Wow your interviewer by saying, "Based on my research, I believe that your company would be a spoon and the one thing every spoon needs is a fork. With soup always comes a salad, no? I'd be a fork."

However you answer, don't stress out! Take a deep breath. Pause for a moment. Show that you've researched the company, that you're the best candidate for the job, that you're cool under pressure. As Han Solo says, "I don't know. Fly casual."

When in doubt, pivot and redirect. Pivoting is a technique commonly used to dodge a question in a diplomatic way. Pivot when an interviewer asks you a question you don't feel entirely comfortable answering, whatever the reason may be. Experts in pivoting do it subtly enough that the interviewer hardly notices the shift in conversation. Watch political debates and you'll see politicians doing this with great skill.

For example, let's say an interviewer asks you about a gap in your employment and you don't really want to reveal that during that year you were going through a divorce and wallowing in your sorrows at a tropical island retreat. This is when pivoting can be useful. Respond by saying, "That was a time in my life when I was doing personal exploration and it ultimately led me to apply to the MBA program from which I just graduated."

Asking a question in return is also a skillful way to pivot. "Have you ever wished you could just take a year off and hide out on a tropical island? Well, I was taking advantage of a period in my life when I could do just that." Pivot to avoid responding to challenging questions when you don't want to divulge the entire back story or share experiences that you feel are too personal.

Use nonverbal factors to influence others. Did you know that your words account for only seven percent of how people judge you? It's true. Body language and presentation are the most significant ways people make assumptions about who you are. In a job interview, planning and preparation are important, but nothing compares to showing confidence as you head into that room. Your interviewer will decide how competent and likable you are in a fraction of a second, so your body language and facial expressions are crucial to your success. (See the chapter resource list for several links to tips on projecting powerful nonverbal cues.)

Use body language to influence yourself. Amy Cuddy, a social psychologist and an associate professor at Harvard Business School, has spent years studying the power of our bodies to change our minds. She says that not only do you have to fake it until you make it, but she also encourages you to "fake it until you become it."

According to Cuddy, if our nonverbal actions govern how we think and feel about ourselves, they undoubtedly affect how others see us. So it's important to be in control of our nonverbal cues in any social situation, but especially in an interview.

Stay curious. Most experts agree that employers love a candidate who is intellectually curious. When explaining how you solved a problem at a previous job, give examples of how you used your curiosity to fix it. This shows employers that not only are you an inquisitive individual, but that you know how to use it to your advantage and, most importantly, to their advantage.

Those questions you prepared before the interview? Now's the time to ask them. Almost every interview ends with the question, "Do you have any questions for me?" Show your preparation and interest in the position by asking away.

Learn how the job selection process works. When you ask your interviewer what happens next, it empowers you. It's also a question most employers expect interview candidates to ask. Ask for a detailed description of the decision-making process once the first round of interviews is complete.

Finally—and most importantly—ask for the job! Do not end that interview without saying how much you want the job. "Thank you for your time. I want you to know that I am very excited about this position and that I really want this job! When can I expect to hear from you?" In sales there's the old saying, "Always make the 'ask' and attempt to close the sale," and this is true in an interview, too.

Wait—you're not finished yet!

What you do after the interview is almost as important as what you did during it. Seal the deal with your post-interview follow-up.

How to Get Personal (But Not Too Personal!) After the Interview

by **Deena Pierott**, Recruiting, Onboarding, Diversity, and Inclusion Consultant

After an interview, you want to stay top of mind with the prospective employer. That requires appropriate, professional follow-up. Don't let that hiring manager forget who you are and that you're interested in the position—but also know when enough is enough!

The first thing I tell people is to do the old-school thing: write a thank-you card. Don't send an email; do it the old-fashioned way, with ink, paper, and a postage stamp! Write your note as soon as the interview is over and mail it the same day. If you were interviewed by a panel, make sure you get everybody's business cards so you can write each person an individual thank-you card.

If you have an inside connection within the organization—particularly someone who is a current employee—this is the time to give a status update. Let your contact know how your interview went and ask him or her to put a good word in for you. Hiring managers listen to their employees, and you might have an inside advantage by having that person vouch for you.

Some people recommend connecting with the interviewer on LinkedIn immediately after an interview. I actually don't encourage this practice. Instead, I would wait until after a job offer has been made before sending invitations to connect on social media. Even if you don't get the job, you may want to connect on LinkedIn and Twitter, as these connections may help you in your ongoing search. Just send a simple note saying, "It was a great experience interviewing with you. Even though I did not receive the position, I would still like to stay in touch."

If you haven't heard anything for three or four days after the interview, send an email to the recruiter or HR representative who was your first point of contact at the organization. Do not contact the hiring manager right off the bat. If that recruiter is not available, then follow up with the hiring manager directly. Be polite in your communications. A simple probe such as "I had a great experience and was wondering where you are in the hiring process?" will probably get you the information you're looking for.

When it comes to follow-up, always make two attempts. If you don't hear back after two emails, it's a sign.

In the cases where you don't get the job, ask for feedback. Many hiring managers or recruiters can offer constructive advice for your ongoing search. You can often learn more about yourself as a job candidate from their comments than you did in the original interview.

And one more thing—don't forget to alert your references. Remember how in Chapter 5 we told you to check in with your references after you have an interview? Well, now is the time to do it. If you think it is likely that your interviewer will be in touch (and even if you don't think it's likely), it's a good idea to touch base with your references. Tell them about the job you interviewed for, the person you interviewed with, and which of your skills and experience you would like them to emphasize if the interviewer calls them. Don't forget to thank them—again!—for acting as your reference.

Don't forget to negotiate!

Got a job offer? Congratulations! Now get ready to negotiate. Don't forget. . .

You need to know local salary ranges for the position. Many factors influence the salaries, including education and local cost of living. We should all take one step when considering a salary offer—know what the local market pays. Below are four national websites to help you learn what your coworkers and professional peers earn. In addition many other resources will often help you identify local and regional salary ranges in your field. A quick Internet search should help you get more specific.

- **Glassdoor.com:** This site collects data from employees on their salaries, benefits, and office culture. Search for information based on location, company, and job title.
- **Bureau of Labor Statistics:** This U.S. government website maintains wage data by area and occupation on a national level.
- **National Council of Nonprofits—Research, Reports, and Data on the Nonprofit Sector:** This site includes data for the nonprofit sector as well as economic impact reports.
- **USA.gov:** This is a good resource to find out about pay and benefits for federal employees.

It's a process that depends on give and take. Be reasonable, of course, but know that most employers expect you to negotiate on salary, benefits, and other issues. When possible, try to negotiate additional salary or benefits when the opportunity presents itself. Here are three techniques to use in your salary negotiations:

- **You need to separate the people from the problem.** Salary is a very personal matter, so emotions like fear, frustration, or anger can arise. Addressing the issues without damaging the relationship is the most important goal. So first try to understand the source of any emotions that come up. Work to address the root of the feeling (underappreciation, a misunderstanding, etc.).

  Before you go into a negotiation, carefully examine the company's or manager's point of view, including goals and obstacles. Knowing the other side's perspective is crucial to negotiation and can help you to distance yourself from issues that might at first seem personal.

Communication in negotiation is important. Be an active listener and occasionally summarize the other person's points by saying, "So what I hear you say is. . ." to sidestep misunderstandings. Avoid reacting, take your time, breathe, and don't be afraid to sit in silence while you think out your talking points before you speak.

- **Focus on interests, not positions.** In their book *Getting to Yes*, Roger Fisher and William Ury explain that positioning yourself on a number or an outcome at the start puts the other party on the defensive, which can be a roadblock to successful negotiation. Avoid this trap by explaining your interests and giving the other person the opportunity to do the same.

  An interest could be something like, "I want to feel that I'm valued here," or "Quality of life is really important to me." Pay attention to their interests, too, and work toward creative solutions that fulfill the interests and needs of both parties, or find places where there might be an opportunity for mutual benefit.

  If an employer won't budge on salary, consider asking for the chance to work from home once a month, for a cellphone reimbursement or a bus pass, or for whatever creative solutions you feel will help to meet your needs or promote your interests. These might be ways for you to compromise in some areas where your supervisor has wiggle room.

- **Ask for more time to think about it.** This might be the greatest tip of all. Negotiation can be exhausting and there might be some back and forth, so don't hesitate to ask for a day or two to think about it. Give a specific time when you'll have a decision, consider the offer, and if you want to continue negotiations, ask for another meeting to discuss.

  If you walk into a negotiation and you feel blind as to what to expect from your boss or new employer, get his or her side and then ask for time to think about it. Say you need to speak with your spouse or partner, your mentor, or whomever (it doesn't matter), and go home and consider your options.

  By all means, if they shove a piece of paper at you with a number on it, don't sign right away. Give yourself some time to noodle on it. If you feel you've been underbid right from the start and they won't budge on anything, ask for the opportunity to renegotiate your salary, benefits, or contract in six months. It can't hurt.

Four Tips on How to Negotiate Like a Pro

by **Jeff Weiss**, President of Lesley University and author of
Harvard Business Review's Guide to Negotiating

1. Know your "why's." People often think of negotiations in terms of their wants: they want more money, or more vacation time, or a new job title. Being clear on your wants is important. But even more important is knowing why you want these things. For example, do you want more money to make a down payment on a house? Or to pay off student loans? Or to invest in your retirement fund? It's the "why's" that you want to satisfy in negotiation and the "why's" that give you more creativity and flexibility in negotiation.

Employers have "why's" on their side as well. There are reasons why they need to protect some things and achieve other things, and why they therefore might be more flexible in one area of compensation and less flexible in others. Figure out the interests on both sides of the table and you'll find fruitful areas for negotiation.

2. Don't fall into stereotypical thinking. Often, we think about negotiation as a haggle, where each side makes demands—one high and one low—and they eventually meet somewhere in the middle. "I'm going to ask for an X% raise, they're going to offer a Y% raise, and we're going to compromise on a Z% raise." That kind of linear, zero-sum thinking limits your opportunity to find creative solutions that work for both parties.

Again, we get back to "why." Perhaps your employer can't give you the paycheck you're asking for, but can address your underlying need for money. For example, let's say you are looking for more money for tuition to go back to school at night. Your employer may be willing to directly cover your tuition, provide you with a low-interest loan, or put you on an assignment and with a mentor who might be able to help you develop the desired knowledge or skills. The trick is to share your interests and then get creative.

Instead of haggling, aim to engage in joint problem-solving. Start with brain-storming ("How might we get this done?"). Try to develop many possible solutions, or what are often called "options," together. Invent first, evaluate later. In the end, you may find that where you end up actually provides you with more value—and meets your interests even better—than what you originally had in your head as your opening request.

3. Avoid emotionally driven ultimatums. People can get reactive during a negotiation. Your manager might say, "This is the most I can do," or, "If you don't like it, you can look somewhere else," or "We've never done that before." These kinds of comments aren't always meant to be tactics or dirty tricks, but they can often feel that way. Don't react in kind.

Instead, take a step back, think about what the person is saying, and respond with good questions. For example, if your manager says, "We've never done it that way before" or "we've never paid that much," you might constructively respond, "Is that so? Has no one here ever gotten a raise/been paid this much? Truly no one?" Don't let them off the hook, but wait for a response. If there have been exceptions, ask, "What have those exception been? What were the reasons for those exceptions?" Ask questions that explore both parties' interests, but that, as much as possible, get at objective standards. Press for past practices, precedents, objective criteria, relevant data, and fair processes. If you want to change the game, one very effective way to do so is to move the conversation from what one should do (that is subjective) to what one ought to do (based on something objective).

4. Take the lead. More than half of people in a negotiation wait for the other party to go first, and shape their approach to what their counterpart does. Don't make this your default. By starting the discussion, you have the opportunity to frame the discussion in a positive, constructive way. Rather than throwing out competing numbers in an emotionally charged haggle session, you can have a constructive conversation around interests, options, and objective standards. Leading the conversation in this direction benefits you, not only in terms of outcome, but also in demonstrating to your employer that you are a skilled negotiator and problem-solver.

Dig deeper!

For links to some of the topics covered in this chapter (including sample interview questions, pivoting and body language during job interviews, and salary information, among many others), go to www.macslist.org/references.

7 Creating and Marketing Your Brand

As you look for work and build your career, it's important to develop your personal brand. Your brand is what helps you stand out in the marketplace. It's a (sometimes intangible) combination of your work experience, professional and personal interests, and areas of expertise. Embrace your passions, quirks, and differences and make them a part of why people want to hire you.

Create your personal brand.

After a certain amount of time, most major metropolitan cities can feel like a small town, once you factor in your different circles, such as neighborhoods, professional groups, the arts, sports, and other community interests. Spend enough time in one place and you'll find that while everyone may not know your name, they probably know someone else who does. And guess what? You have a personal brand whether you like it or not—and even if you're not sure exactly what it is.

Creating and developing your brand is useful at any stage of your career. It can be helpful when you are just starting out, as part of an overall self-evaluation (as described in Chapter 1), or as a means of making your first job a successful one. As you gain more job experience, personal branding plays an important role in helping you stand out in a crowded marketplace.

Start off on the right foot. When you finally land that job—either your first, a new one in a different field, or as a return after a hiatus—you want to begin by creating a reputation as a top-notch professional. It's important to fit in and make the most of every opportunity. A successful brand starts with solid skills, great work experience, and fabulous word of mouth.

- **Be a savvy newbie.** Offer an outsider's perspective and raise new questions. But don't come on too strong or project too much of a "know-it-all" vibe for a beginner.

- **Be a social butterfly.** Set up get-acquainted meetings, coffees, or lunches with new coworkers and clients. They will teach you a lot and appreciate your curiosity.
- **Be a listener.** Yes, you have a lot to offer. But so do your new colleagues and customers. Listen to what they say about their problems and their ideas for fixing them.
- **Be the office historian.** Look ahead, not back, but understand where your organization has been. Talk to supervisors and colleagues about previous challenges faced by your new company and your predecessors. If you can, tap the wisdom and experience of others who have already done your job or similar ones.
- **Be an expert in the field.** Are you working in a central office or support function like communications or human resources? Get out into the field and talk to the people who provide the product you produce and to the people you serve. Learn everything you can about your new line of work.
- **Be an early achiever.** Try to identify an urgent need to solve in the first six months. Getting a big accomplishment under your belt quickly gives you credibility and authority.

Analyze your strengths and values. As you gain work experience and hone your skills, you are learning more about your abilities and interests. What do you like doing? What are you good at? What don't you like to do? What would you like to learn more about? Adding new abilities and areas of interest to your core skill set helps to expand your brand outside the confines of your job description and takes you in the direction you want to go.

Your Uniqueness, Your Threads

by **Aubrie De Clerck**, Owner of Coaching for Clarity

As we advance through our career, it is up to us to tell our story—the story of who we are, what we can do, and how we stand out doing it. Our story is not simply about identifying transferable skills. To find fulfilling work, we need to communicate our threads—the things we are best at, the things we can't stop doing if we try, the things we do naturally, our gifts.

Using your threads as a foundation for your search builds confidence, both within yourself and with employers. It simplifies your messaging for resumes, cover letters, and LinkedIn, while preparing you for interviews. Threads can also help you understand what questions you need to ask to find out whether a particular role would be fulfilling.

To get a sense of threads, let's take a common transferable skill, problem solving, and go a few steps further. Being a problem solver is great, but many people solve problems. This skill alone won't help you stand out. You'll need to narrow in on your special brand of problem solving. You can start with these questions:

What specifically?

What kinds of problems do you solve? People, data, organizational? Problems that take many years to solve, or ones you can check off a list each day?

Example: I resolve complex customer service issues.

In what way?

Is there a particular way that you solve problems that is unique to you? Have you received positive feedback from others about the kinds of contributions you have made?

Example (continued): I resolve complex customer service issues with patience and persistence.

To what end?

Is there a particular outcome to solving the problem that you are trying to achieve? Does the solution need to work in one instance or always work?

Example (continued even further): I resolve complex customer service issues with patience and persistence, resulting in concrete, repeatable solutions.

So what do we know about the example problem solver?

This person would be fulfilled by:

- solving challenging, multifaceted people problems,
- having the time to understand the issue and craft a solution,
- and making sure the problems do not continue in the future.

An employer could expect:

- a thorough, driven employee
- increased operational efficiency as problems are solved
- satisfied customers

What questions could this person ask employers to evaluate whether he or she wants a certain job?

- What kinds of problems do you solve for customers?
- How long does it typically take to resolve customer problems?
- Are there recurring problems? If so, how are they handled?

Now it's your turn. Pick a transferable skill you enjoy using and run it through this process. Start building your foundation for not only an easier search but also for more compelling conversations about your unique gifts at any point in your career.

Promote your personal brand.

Once you've identified your personal threads and decided what they can contribute in your chosen field, you need to articulate that brand through unified messaging.

Social media: What you do and say on social media can strengthen or weaken your personal brand. Are you a job seeker with a bare-bones LinkedIn profile? You are sending a message to employers that you aren't serious about your profession. What are you saying on Twitter that employers or colleagues might learn about you? Social media is a huge contributor to your personal brand.

Positioning statement: This is how we want our audience to perceive, think, and feel about us versus the competition. Want to work in public relations for an art museum? Great! The more you understand your audience, the better you will be at positioning yourself for that new job. Think of it this way: To (target audience)—I'm the applicant who offers (benefit) over others in this field. The reason is that (explain how your experiences or features relate to the benefit you can provide).

Vision statement: This statement allows you to see where you are now and where you intend to be. This is what's called an internal communications piece—

only for you to keep in the back of your mind. According to *The Science and Art of Branding* by Giep Franzen and Sandra Moriarty, "A vision statement is what a brand wants to be in the future and it consists of the brand's purpose and values." A solid vision for the future should guide you in setting your professional and life goals.

Elevator pitch: This is a very practical piece to nail down when looking for a job or networking. Create a concise and efficient elevator pitch that is an effective and memorable way to articulate your personal brand to new acquaintances. Walk the fine line between humility and confidence, but communicate your personal brand in an engaging way that gives a lasting first impression.

Professional bio: Whether it appears on your LinkedIn page, resume, or cover letter, a professional summary is your opportunity to use the keywords that define your personal brand. It typically draws upon your positioning and visioning statements to come up with a succinct narrative that distinguishes your personal brand from the competition.

Mike Russell of Pivotal Writing, a creator of content-marketing materials for online software companies, has also written about professional bios. Here are his top three suggestions for crafting a bio that will connect with future employers and clients:

- **Know your target audience.** Are you looking for nonprofit work? Maybe your passion is the environment? Or do you want to make a ton of money selling software? You must identify and speak to the audience you want to attract. As Mike says, "Speak as if you were addressing your ideal customer."

- **Talk to your target audience—this is not about you.** You must show how you can help your audience. "Shift the tone of your bio 10 degrees," says Mike, "and you can really change the effectiveness of your message." This is the difference between features and benefits—show how your "features" will "benefit" the target audience.

- **Leave a lasting impression.** "What is the one story that you want readers to remember after reading your bio?" asks Mike. Connect with the reader in an authentic way and you will distinguish yourself from your competition.

Website: Your website is an important part of your brand. It's a great place to advertise yourself and to refer potential clients and employers when they want to learn more about you. With a little time and effort, you can boost your professional presence online dramatically.

Here are four ways you can use a personal website to promote your brand.

- **Show and tell.** Your own website allows you to present information in greater depth than you can on your resume. With an online platform you can show past projects and writing samples and give a future employer the chance to see the details of what you have done.

- **Stay up to date.** Save time by refreshing your site and sharing your work right away. Provide an updated link to different prospective employers, or notify your LinkedIn followers that you have added something new to your webpage.

- **Share your personality.** A personal website allows for artistic freedom, and you can tailor it to your personal traits and preferences. Create a unique layout or logo, or provide an in-depth bio about yourself. This shows employers and future clients your taste and gives a sense of who you are.

- **Learn a new trade.** Launching and maintaining a website teaches you marketable technical skills. Popular publishing platforms like WordPress are easy to use, but you still need know how to work with Cascading Style Sheets (CSS) and other online tools. Learning these techniques shows employers that you can teach yourself and catch on quickly. (Or, check out the free website-building sites listed in the chapter resource list.)

Visuals: You need to brand everything related to you and your career, whether it is your resume, your cover letter, your portfolio, your business card, your bio, or your website, with a consistent visual presentation. The unified look helps to reinforce your brand wherever it is referenced. The following are three areas where your materials need to be consistent, clean, and appealing.

- **Color:** Pick a strong—but not overwhelming—color to use throughout the key materials that represent your personal brand. William Arruda, founder of REACH Personal Branding, suggests this scale to help choose the right color:

  Use **red** to express action, passion, power, or courage.

  Use **orange** to express determination, encouragement, strength, or productivity.

  Use **yellow** to express optimism, positivity, energy, or vision.

  Use **green** to express the environment, calmness, growth, or rebirth.

Use **blue** to express trust, reliability, integrity, or truth.

Use **purple** to express luxury, spirituality, inspiration, or dignity.

To use color effectively in your materials, pick a signature area to do so and keep it simple. Common ways to incorporate color on your resume include underlining your name or having all of your job titles in your chosen color.

- **Font:** Choosing a signature font for your materials can be very beneficial to your brand. Make sure it is easy to read; serif fonts, with their curves and hooks have more personality, but can sometimes be hard to read. Avoid gimmicky fonts (hello, Comic Sans) or ones that may become dated too quickly.

- **Format:** The format of your resume, cover letter, business card, e-portfolio, and even website (to whatever extent possible) needs to be consistent for your personal brand to ring clear. Font, color, and placement need to be the same throughout all materials. For example, if your resume has a vertical header with your name and contact information, then your other materials should have the same.

Turn your brand into self-employment.

As you develop your personal brand, you may find yourself succeeding so well at self-promotion that you begin to consider self-employment. Or you may have just become tired of working for someone else or of looking for the perfect job that never quite materializes. For many people, self-employment is a great alternative to working inside a company or other organization.

Self-employment allows for a more flexible lifestyle and a routine that can exist outside the rigid nine-to-five workday. Whether it is part-time freelancing, a series of temporary full-time projects, or a full-time brick-and-mortar business, self-employment allows for more diversity in how you budget your time and money.

As with a job hunt, deciding to become self-employed requires some in-depth self-assessment and soul searching. Many resources can guide you if you choose this path, but here are a few do's and don'ts to consider up front.

Do...

- **Analyze the market.** You really, really, really need to understand the market—whether it is local, national, or international—for your goods or services. The only way to position and promote the value and benefits you bring to that market is to first know it inside and out.

- **Make friends with your competitors.** Even though you're competing in a general way, you've all got your own individual niches. So play nice. It's good karma. It's also good business. Remember, your colleagues and competitors will be the first to refer you when they have overflow business or projects.

- **Brand yourself early on.** Branding is especially important in self-employment. Become the "go-to" person in your specialized field and then make that a prominent part of your brand. This is your way of standing out in that market you've just gotten to know so well.

- **Create a solid business plan.** Sometimes people ease their way into self-employment by starting with a side business—freelancing projects, selling something at a local market, or teaching a class. That's great, but once you decide to invest a lot of time and money into your business, you need a detailed financial plan. Work with a professional planner or have it reviewed by one. Your bottom line will thank you.

- **Budget carefully.** As you eagerly calculate your future earnings and dream of rolling around on a giant pile of cash, don't forget about the benefits that your former employer may have been paying on your behalf. . . benefits such as health insurance, a retirement program, and— oh yes—the other half of your FICA contribution that you will now have to pay in full. If possible, create a cash reserve to tide you through several months. You need operating funds, and cash flow can become a major issue, especially if clients or customers don't pay you on time.

- **Know yourself and your work habits.** It's time to get real about what you can reasonably expect of yourself. Are you a night person? Then please don't set up a work schedule that regularly requires you to work early mornings. Likewise, don't plan to work alone at home if you know you need outside stimulation or if you're afraid you'll spend the entire day napping.

- **Create a schedule.** Sure, you left your nine-to-five job to avoid the daily routine, but you still need a schedule. Sometimes it's the only thing that keeps you from spending the entire afternoon watching cute animal videos on YouTube. Try to plan your days and weeks so that you allow time for the work tasks themselves, in addition to other activities such as networking, self-promotion, client contact, communications. . . and a life outside work.

- **Prepare to work more than you expect.** See above. Then double the amount of time you think you're going to need. Self-employment brings with it a huge amount of unpaid hidden or "shadow" work, such as managing employees, interacting with customers, attracting new business, keeping track of hours and inventory, invoicing, banking, paying taxes, and doing a wide variety of other administrative tasks.

Don't. . .

- **Start a business if you're afraid of taking risks.** Remember that part about knowing yourself? There's no shame in being risk averse. But if you're planning to be self-employed, at least part of your nature needs to be willing to take the leap and embrace your inner daredevil, if only in a controlled and cautious fashion. If not, you may want to choose a more secure career path. (However, do know that many experts believe that in the long run, self-employment offers the least overall career risk—you never have to fear being fired, laid off, or tortured by an incompetent boss who makes you so crazy you quit in despair.)

- **Try to do too much too fast.** Self-employment is exciting. You're doing what you want to do and doing it on your own terms. But things can change quickly. It's easy to get in over your head and not be able to handle the work in a timely fashion. Remember, you want your personal brand to stand for quality, reliability, and integrity, not "Uh, I meant to get that to you last week—how does first thing Monday morning sound?" Be fastidious about meeting deadlines and delivery dates.

- **Put all your eggs in one basket.** (Or at least don't do it without being aware of the potential downside.) Whenever possible, diversify. Try to get a broad base of clients. That way, if a client suddenly loses a budget line or a sector of the economy takes a turn for the worse, you won't lose all your income in one fell swoop. That said, if you are making tons of money from a single source, congratulations! Don't fret about it too much, but do keep your eyes open to expanding your customer base whenever possible.

- **Isolate.** Even if you are a one-person show, you still need ideas, advice, and social contact. Make time to reach out to colleagues and other self-employed professionals, whether it is during an informal get-together or at a professional networking event.

Depending on where you live, there may be additional taxes for the self-employed (such as a city business license or other county and local taxes), so you need to plan for those as well. And, as mentioned previously, the self-employed also pay both the employee and employer share of the federal FICA tax that funds Social Security and Medicare, instead of just the employee portion. A good bookkeeper or accountant can help you get a handle on your tax situation before it's time to file your tax forms. Remember, no one likes an ugly surprise come April!

Finally, if you're self-employed, you need to think about your own retirement savings, such as a Simplified Employee Pension (SEP) or a 401(k) plan. The type of plan depends on what kind of business you set up. An accountant or retirement investment specialist can let you know which option is best for you.

Still having trouble deciding if self employment is right for you? Talk to other people who have made the leap. Their stories can help shape your decision.

Taking the Big Leap into Self-Employment

by **Mac Prichard,** Founder of Mac's List and Prichard Communications

Some people grow up in families of business owners and can't imagine working for anybody else. Others start a lemonade stand, paper route, or lawn service and launch a full-time business after finishing school. And many employees develop entrepreneurial skills inside organizations and then strike out on their own.

Ten years ago I joined the last group.

I've always had a job outside the home since childhood, but I didn't open the doors of my first business, Prichard Communications, until 2007. And it wasn't until three years later that I hired my first employee at my second business, Mac List.

Before I became an employer I spent almost 30 years working for public agencies, nonprofits, and elected officials. I enjoyed those jobs very much.

In fact, I might still be working for someone else, except that one day I received a call from a favorite boss. Her national foundation funded my communications job at a juvenile justice reform project. She knew my job would end soon. Would I like to start my own public relations firm with her as my first client?

The truth is I'd never thought of myself as a small business owner. But the projects my client and I discussed were exciting and involved the social-change work I love to do. I knew I had the necessary skills. As the veteran of more than a dozen political campaigns, I'd gotten good at building enterprises from scratch and enjoyed managing them, too.

Striking out on your own is scary, whether you're just working for yourself or hiring employees. How do you know if you're up to the challenge?

You're ready to start your own business if you can say yes to one or more of the following:

1. You've had lots of experience setting up and running projects, events, or side hustles.

2. You know what you want to do and whom you want to serve.

3. You understand your customer's problems and how you can solve them.

In my case, I could answer yes to all three questions. My time in government and local politics had taught me how to build and run successful programs that got results. I also knew that I was passionate about helping social-change organizations communicate their missions and accomplishments. Finally, I understood the needs of the customers I wanted to serve and how to help them.

My public relations agency, Prichard Communications, celebrates its tenth anniversary in 2017. I'm fortunate to have a great team and great clients. We work exclusively with nonprofits, foundations, and purpose-driven brands that make the world a better place. It's a privilege to serve such inspiring organizations. Every day at the office brings meaning and deep personal satisfaction.

If you're interested in starting your own business, you need to read Chris Guillebeau's *The $100 Startup* and Eric Ries's *The Lean Startup*. Both books were instrumental in helping me grow Prichard.

You should also talk to people who have done it. Take business owners to lunch. Join professional groups or go to networking events for entrepreneurs, freelancers, or other self-employed people. You will be surprised by how generous others are with their ideas and time.

Never stop learning. Many resources exist for people looking to set up their own businesses. Make sure you do as much research as you can before you make that leap! Take time to check out these resources:

- *The $100 Startup.* Chris Guillebeau writes about unconventional work, entrepreneurship, and foreign travel on his blog, The Art of Nonconformity. He has never held a regular job. Instead, he has found ways to turn his ideas into income that allows him to help others and travel frequently. As Mac mentions above, his book, *The $100 Startup: Reinvent the Way You Make a Living, Do What You Love, and Create a New Future*, offers case studies, practical tips, and well-organized materials useful to everyone who wants find a way to get paid for doing what they love.

- **Making It Anywhere:** In this blog Mish Slade and Rob Dix write about their story and how to run a business from anywhere in the world.

- **MediaBistro:** This job list sites offers career advice for media professionals. It has a section on going freelance as well as professional resume-writing services.

Dig deeper!

For links to some of the topics covered in this chapter (including first-job tips, personal branding, free website-building tools, and taking a leap of faith, among many others), go to www.macslist.org/references.

8 Navigating Your Career Path

Think of your career as a long, never-ending highway project. But unlike those construction delays, you can actually control your career's direction, movement, and timing. Even when work gets stressful and you can feel the demands piling up, it's good to poke your head up occasionally and take a look around. Remind yourself that your career is constantly moving and evolving. You can take it along the road you choose and, with any luck, avoid most of the potholes along the way.

Make conscious decisions about your goals.

Once you find a job and then maybe another one or two, it's easy to settle into a routine. And that's fine—as we all know, job hunting is stressful and you deserve a chance to relax and bask in the joy of your fabulous new career. Suddenly you have interesting professional responsibilities, fascinating coworkers, and. . . an income! Hooray! Life is good.

But after some time has passed and the novelty wears off, you may find yourself wondering, "Is this it?" Maybe you want to explore other areas. Maybe your new job is a bit more stressful or time-consuming than you had hoped. Maybe it's not a good fit for your personal strengths and weaknesses. Or maybe you've just outgrown it.

Never stop assessing yourself and your values. The key to happiness in any career is to find an organization that shares your values and a job that allows you to use your strengths. In your career path, it is easy to forget that you, as the employee, are evaluating the company as much they are evaluating you. It's like dating—will this relationship be a good fit long term?

Is quality of life more important to you than a large paycheck? Do you hate teamwork? Do you love networking or dislike sitting in an office? Do you want to do different things every day? Take the time to return to and answer the tough questions you learned to ask yourself back in Chapter 1.

If you are looking for a career that does more than pay the rent or mortgage, you need a more holistic approach to your career strategy. Kare Anderson, former *Wall Street Journal* reporter, addressed this issue in a talk hosted by the University of Oregon School of Journalism and Communications. Her advice? Build a set of values from which you operate and use them to guide you on your career path. Here are Kare's values for crafting a career:

- **"The sooner we get clearer about our top talent, the quicker we can hone it and offer value."** Figure out your top strength—what you have to offer the world—and refine it. Home in on it. Applying for jobs willy-nilly isn't a great idea. Be strategic about where you can use your talents and for what cause.

- **"Find allies. It's a hybrid world, so befriend people who have different talents than you."** Once you know your top talent, connect with others to understand where they shine. Ask questions. Be curious. You never know what you'll find out. Connect them with others. Share information. Help them and look for ways that they can help you. We'll all be better for it, and it could lead to opportunities you've never considered.

- **"Find the sweet spot of mutual benefit sooner rather than later."** Look for the intersection of your talent with the talents of others, find mutual benefit, and innovate together for a more resourceful approach to your mission.

- Ask: **"Whom do you draw closer to you? Whom do you admire the most and how do you honor them? Are you a giver, a taker, or a matcher?"** Use these questions as a way to guide strategy for your career and your life goals.

Ask yourself, "What makes work meaningful?" If having meaningful work is one of your values, remember that meaningful work can mean different things to different people. To understand what it looks like for you, ask yourself these questions:

- **What if working to put food on the table for you and your family may, in fact, make work meaningful?** You can find meaning in the results you produce, the coworkers you interact with, the mission you support, or the sheer fact that the money you make allows you to take care of your loved ones and yourself. Even the ability to pay off a large debt can give a job more meaning.

- What if meaningful work is only an abstract concept that may elicit any combination of feelings such as satisfaction, comfort, gratitude, relief, stability, power, or influence at any given time? Maybe your job isn't helping to save the rain forests or feed the homeless, but maybe it's helping you feel more secure? In your security, you might find that you're happier, kinder, and more thoughtful to your loved ones, which gives your life more meaning.

- Is meaningful work found in the opportunity to use your best strengths and talents? Tom Rath, author of *StrengthsFinder 2.0*, argues that when you do work that allows you to use your strengths, you're happier, more productive, and feel more satisfaction at the end of the day.

- Maybe meaningful work is a combination of all these ideas and concepts and it's up to us to figure out whether we're content in our present situation or if we long for more? If so, what does more look like? Sometimes, as the poet Rainer Maria Rilke wrote, you have to "live the questions" to find the answers you seek. The longing for meaningful work is indeed a personal quest, unique to you and your own set of circumstances.

Four Principles to Guide Your Career

by **Ben Forstag**, Managing Director of Mac's List

Careers develop continuously over the forty or fifty years of our working lives. They are subject to forces both internal (family dynamics, changes of interest) and external (the economy, the job market). Accordingly, I've always been dubious about "mapping out" an entire career in advance. The linear progressions of model career development—law school, clerkship, federal prosecutor, Ninth Circuit, Supreme Court!—rarely play out so cleanly in real life.

I've certainly worked to navigate my career's direction. However, rather than targeting a predetermined destination, I've focused on the journey itself. My career plan is less a roadmap than it is a set of four practical guiding principles.

1. Do what you're good at. We've all heard the dictum "do what you love." This is great advice if you have strong passions and a clear vision of how to monetize them. But sometimes the things we love most don't translate into a job that pays the bills—at least not right away. In these situations, I urge people to focus first on their skills, rather than their passions—do what you do well!

Skills can transfer to different jobs, industries, and interests. Focusing on professional strengths gives you career flexibility, while also illuminating potential avenues for work in the field of your choice. Ultimately, passion and skill are two sides of the same coin. You are good at some things and not others for a reason; your skill set is a reflection of the interest and enjoyment you derive from those activities. In this sense, doing what you're good at is actually a way to do what you love.

2. Keep learning. Taken by itself, the "do what you're good at" rule could lead to a static, monotonous career. That's why it's important to stay curious and explore new interests and skills. Read books and blogs, take classes, network outside your field—do anything that exposes you to new ideas. You may discover professional interests that you never imagined.

Throughout my own career I have tried to say "yes" to learning opportunities whenever they appear. As a result, I've gained new passions for statistics, data analytics, and coding—a surprising development for someone who went out of his way to avoid math classes in college!

3. Stay balanced. It's good to be passionate about your job, but it's also important to have passions outside of the office. One of the best things you can do for your career is to have a healthy work-life balance that provides an escape valve for the stresses of work. It can also insulate you from the inevitable down periods in your professional life.

4. Live your own dream. This is the final rule, but perhaps the most important. You have to evaluate your career according to your own criteria—not anyone else's. Measuring yourself against other people's successes is like trying to live their dream, rather than your own. Try to focus on what you want and like to do without worrying about what others may think. Professional contentment is neither objective nor relative; the only question is whether your job and career path bring you happiness.

Create your career path. Then follow it. (Or vice versa.)

Analyze before acting. Sometimes you create your career path up front and follow it according to plan. Other times you look back at your footsteps and see that they have created a path of their own. Either way, at some point you need to stop and reflect on where you've been and where you're going.

Dawn Rasmussen (who offered some great reasons to network in Chapter 3) has written a guide to career management, *Forget Job Security: Build Your Marketability!, Finding Job Success in the New Era of Career Management.* Her focus is on how to foolproof your career in a volatile and fickle job market. Here are six steps she recommends you take to manage your career:

- **Define your purpose.** You need to know what you want. Being clear about your career goals helps you explain what you offer and ultimately helps you answer the question every employer asks, "What can you do for me?"

- **Know your value.** Successful career managers can explain the unique value they offer with a short statement that connects with an employer's wants, needs, and values.

- **Develop your brand.** If you don't develop a personal brand, employers and colleagues will do it for you. You need to identify your passions, strengths, and skills, and turn these lists into a branding statement you can use in interviews and presentations.

- **Master the building blocks.** Everybody has to have a few basic career building blocks in place. These include adding new skills, paying attention to your reputation (especially online), and building value inside and outside an organization.

- **Keep your tools current.** Good career managers regularly update their resumes, work samples, and other application materials. They see these documents as dynamic and so are ready when an unexpected opportunity presents itself.

- **Shape your destiny.** Think and plan ahead. Be prepared for new opportunities (or layoffs) by taking classes, participating in industry organizations, mentoring others, and working to a career plan.

Know when it's time to start looking again. The key question to ask yourself is, "Do you feel stuck?" If so, it's time to think about making some changes. While the best decisions we can make for ourselves are also often the hardest, sometimes the most difficult decision you can make is the best decision for you.

Here are five signs that you're stuck and what you can do about it:

- **You feel paralyzed.** Do you pursue jobs, projects, or professional relationships only to be caught between a yes and a no? Do you feel like you're standing in the middle of a foreign town without a map? The inability to make a decision can feel paralyzing. If this is how you feel, stop spinning your wheels, bring your attention to the current events in your life, and ask yourself this: What is holding you back? Go with your gut answer and don't be afraid to acknowledge it (if only to yourself at first).

- **You feel uninspired.** Do you just sit in a chair at the end of the day and stare at the wall? Have you lost interest in doing the things that you once loved? Feeling uninspired can be the result of sadness, grief, and loss, but it can also be a sign that you're stuck. Is fear holding you back from doing what's best for you? Are other people's opinions holding you back? Find a way to overcome your fears, make a change, and prepare for a shift.

- **You feel confused.** A major life decision can be overwhelming and we often see both sides of the coin—the good and bad—equally. This causes us to feel stuck in confusion. Try this: Close your eyes and envision the yes and the no to your question. Which feels lighter, brighter, and more peaceful? Go with that answer. Always. Be prepared for the answer to be the scariest and most difficult to accept.

- **You can't commit to anything.** Do you pursue something only to bail when it gets serious? Better to work through this now and save yourself the grief—something is wrong and needs fixing. So fix it. Be brave and take small steps towards your goal.

- **You're uncomfortable with the status quo.** Signs that you need a change in your life can show up in different ways. They can manifest as anger, sadness, and anxiety. They can also appear as a longing for something different, and jealousy or envy of others. If you're uncomfortable with the status quo, make change by bringing your attention to when you feel angry, sad, or anxious. Once you identify the thing that is causing your pain and needs to change, don't be afraid to take the steps to change it. Set your intention on something better.

Know how to reignite your job search. Once you realize that you are no longer in love with your job, you need to figure out what to do next, and, most importantly, how to keep yourself happy during the process. Navigating a career change isn't easy, but here are some ideas to keep it as smooth as possible:

- **Create a life outside work.** Don't let work be the only thing that is important in your life. Explore the city you're in and find things that allow you to have something to look forward to. Join a cooking class or a book club. Find a hobby for your spare time.

- **Don't be afraid to talk.** Let your close friends and family know you are looking for a career change. Maybe they have some introductions they could make or suggestions for possible opportunities? Contact the college you attended and see how long you have access to its career center. Sit down with an advisor who can help you tweak your resume. Consult with friends. Conduct informational interviews with professionals you know.

- **Look for mentors at your work.** Talk to people you admire. Get ideas from people you trust about how they have gone about their job path.

- **Set goals and work toward them each week.** Map out a plan to get you through your career change. Set attainable goals and do something each week to accomplish them.

- **Set a date for when you want to leave.** Pick a month as a deadline for your exit. This will help you realize that you really are making the change, and it will give you a little push toward getting your job search going.

- **If you want to keep working (as opposed to taking a break), don't leave your job until you have the next one lined up.** Don't find out the hard way that employers prefer to hire people who already have a job. Too many gaps in your resume can raise a red flag for potential employers.

Lessons Learned by the Recently Unemployed

by **Marsha Warner, SPHR**, Founder of Career Factors,
Career Coach, and Executive Recruiter

Recently, a client shared what he wished he'd done before he found himself on the job hunt. Here's a list of best practices for career maintenance that are applicable to everyone:

I wish I'd kept a copy of my performance reviews. *Lesson:* Keep your own file of reviews and accolades. They are helpful to prompt accomplishment statements, to review for interviews, and to remind yourself of achievements when doubts creep in.

I wish I had continued to network and develop outside contacts. *Lesson:* Don't wait until you are unemployed to start networking. Stay in touch with colleagues, classmates, ex-bosses, other parents, fellow volunteers, and so on.

I wish I had joined LinkedIn earlier on. *Lesson:* Keep your LinkedIn profile active. It's a tool for recruiters, a way to stay connected, and a source of information for professional development. Spend an hour a week updating your profile, reconnecting, joining interest groups, and staying current.

I wish I had not taken it so personally; I let this layoff really get to me. *Lesson:* When your job ends, take time to mourn the loss and acknowledge your emotions, then let it go. Know that when you are part of a reduction in force, it's a business decision, not a personal one. Manage what you can control and let go of what you cannot.

I wish I had reached out and passed along my professional knowledge to younger colleagues before I left. *Lesson:* Teaching is a great source of career satisfaction. Some companies have formal programs for knowledge transfer. Seek them out. The effort will be worth the reward you'll feel in sharing your knowledge with others.

I wish I had paid more attention to my own development and taken advantage of challenges that would give me more exposure. *Lesson:* Proactive career management means stepping up to challenges. Volunteering for projects and committees or getting training for new skills are ways to grow. They get you noticed by your boss and bring greater satisfaction to your daily work. Ask yourself at the end of each day, "What did I learn today?"

I wish I had asked for help early on in my job search. Things have changed so much; I feel a bit lost. *Lesson:* Feeling isolated and lost is common. A career coach can offer expert information and advice about the job market and how to put your best foot forward. Portland is blessed with great career resources, including local colleges, private coaches, and job-search support groups. Help is available. Be wise and ask for it.

Position yourself in a changing landscape. What does the "new economy" mean for you and your career? The landscape of getting (and keeping) a job is changing, so you need to pay attention to avoid being left behind. Job seekers need to change the way they talk to employers.

Ask yourself the following questions to keep up with the changing times.

- **How can I add value?** In a *New York Times* op-ed piece by Thomas Friedman entitled "How to Get a Job" (see chapter resource list for the link), Harvard education expert Tony Wagner is quoted on the new paradigm of finding employment: "The world doesn't care what you know, all it cares about is what you can do with what you know." The good news for everyone in today's new world of work is that it's not about where you got your education or how you learned your skills, but about the value you can add to a project or an organization.

- **Do I have the skills?** Today's marketplace is less focused on academic credentials than it is on matching the right skill set with the available work opportunity. This isn't to say you should skip college or graduate school, if you think they are right for you, but the degrees they confer are not enough in today's competitive world of work. Identify the skills you need and then set out to acquire them. Read books on your own time, build relationships with others who are doing similar work, find mentors to guide you on your path, and look for opportunities to gain and practice those skills.

Don't rule out the idea of changing fields. Is it possible to find work in an industry in which you have no experience? The answer is yes. You can definitely move into a new sector and make the case that your skills are transferable. It's never too late to switch fields. The transition can even be easier than you would think and would definitely spark some excitement in your career and your life.

That said, starting your job search in a new field can be intimidating; you may think that employers won't be interested in you due to what they assume is your irrelevant background and work experience. Your mission is to show that your background can still be an asset to your potential employer.

- **Volunteer.** Look for ways to show people what you can do. Join an advisory committee, sign up to help manage an annual dinner, or work on a fundraising drive. This will let leaders see your work firsthand and build important relationships.

- **Network and do informational interviews.** Remember what you learned about this earlier in this guide? It's just as applicable to changing fields as it is to looking for a new job. Reaching out to experts is a great way to find out about the field you hope to enter. Many of the people you meet will also have seen others make the transition into their sector from a different one. Ask what strategies have worked or not worked as they've watched others crack a new field—or better yet, hired such people. And don't forget about professional groups and industry events. Almost every industry or occupation has a professional association. (See the resource list in Chapter 3 for a variety of links to these kinds of groups.)

- **Don't discredit your experience.** Once you begin interviewing in a new field, do not dismiss your own experience—even if it doesn't feel relevant. Every professional experience has value. Recently the hiring manager at Edelman Public Relations in Portland shared a story with the Mac's List staff about someone she interviewed who related her experience as a barista to skills needed in a public relations job. She ended up hiring the barista for a paid internship, based on the case she made. If you can relate your work experience to skills you will need in a future job, it is always valuable.

- **Highlight your personal interests.** Your personal life can boost an employer's opinion of you. Don't be afraid to share what your hobbies and interests are—especially if they demonstrate your creativity or drive. Examples of interests to discuss with an employer might include blogging, photography, running marathons, or volunteering in community events or organizations. Just make sure to focus on how your interests display positive characteristics about you as a potential employee.

Take into account your position and stage in life.

What's right for one person may not be right for the next. And it's true that people in certain demographics—women, minorities, and older and undereducated job seekers, in particular—face specific challenges. It's important to be realistic about the obstacles you face and then try to identify ways to overcome them.

Know your challenges and options. If you find job-hunting difficult due to your demographic identification, try to find ways to preempt or compensate for them whenever possible. Whether it means putting yourself out there in a much more public way (it probably does), getting more training, or hiring a professional to help you polish your image, investing the time and energy now will pay off in the future. Knowledge is power and the more you arm yourself in advance, the better you will weather the difficulties you find in your path. If possible, try to get advice and suggestions from other successful job seekers in your same situation, who can offer the strategies and action steps that worked well for them.

Ageism Is Alive and Well. . . But You Can Fight It!

by **Kerry Hannon**, author of *Love Your Job: The New Rules for Career Happiness*

It is against the law for employers to discriminate based on age. Yet, ageism is an undeniable truth in the modern workforce.

There are several reasons why employers are skeptical of older workers. They worry that you don't have the stamina for the job. They think that you may not be up to speed with technology or willing to learn new things. They anticipate that your salary demands are too high and that your health benefits cost more because of your age. And finally, they question whether you will fit into a culture where you may be reporting to younger bosses.

Here's the good news: there are ways to fight against ageism. Here are my tips:

- **Don't get stuck in the past.** Don't try to simply replace the job you had before. Do some soul-searching to identify your skills and talents. Then explore how how you can redeploy these in a different arena.

- **Get a career coach.** Studies have shown that career coaches are particularly helpful for job seekers over the age of fifty. If you can't afford a coach, you may be able to find one through community colleges or the government's Career One Stop Centers.

- **Consider temporary part-time work.** Just because you're looking for a full-time job doesn't mean you should turn down intermediate work. It keeps your resume alive and puts you out there networking and using your skills.

- **Don't get caught up on salary.** Don't turn down opportunities because you're waiting for the perfect salary. For the right job, you may need to accept lower pay. Think of other benefits: maybe you can get flex time, the chance to telecommute, or extra vacation time.

- **Exercise.** Show you are physically fit—and it doesn't have to mean running fast miles and bench pressing a lot. Employers notice your vitality and vibrancy, and it shows them you are up for the job.

- **Study up on technology.** Take the time to learn about new technologies—either through independent study or by taking courses or workshops.

- **Use social media.** Get active on Twitter, have a LinkedIn profile, and participate in LinkedIn groups. This shows that you're engaged in social media and are at ease with technology. Plus, this is a great way to find new opportunities. Amazingly, many people I worked with twenty years ago have found me on Facebook and have hired me to do work. You never know who your next connection will be.

- **Focus on networking.** Employers still hire people they know or who are referred by people they trust. As an experienced worker, you have a lot of contacts, many more than somebody in their twenties or thirties. So reach out! Dig really deep to find someone who might help you get your foot in the door.

- **Volunteer.** Start engaging and working with nonprofits or other organizations. You might find a job doing skill-based volunteer work. It's a great way to keep your resume alive and fill in gaps.

- **Join (or create) a job-hunting group.** Find people who will keep you accountable to your job search: "What did you do this week? Hey, did you hear about this?" It's really helpful to have a group of people to support you who are also on the same path.

- **Do your homework.** If you want to be in a particular industry, go to meetings and functions that connect you to people and keep your skill set relevant. If you see job descriptions calling for a certain kind of certification, go get it.
- **Believe in yourself.** It's hard when you're struggling to find a job and keep hitting rejection. This is when you need a good circle of people who have your back. Have some confidence and know that there is something out there for you!

Be knowledgeable about reentering the work force. People who take a hiatus—and statistically they are much more likely to be women than men—may find it difficult to return to an equivalent position after a period away from full-time work. This return can be managed, and very successfully, but it pays to plan in advance how you will reenter the work force once you are ready.

How Women Can Make a Successful Return to the Workplace

by **Farai Chideya**, author of *The Episodic Career: How to Thrive at Work in the Age of Disruption*

Women are much more likely than men to leave the workforce to raise children or assist elderly family members. Unfortunately, after a prolonged time off, it's not easy to on-ramp back into full employment. There simply is not much infrastructure to help women step back into the workforce. That's why it's so important to be prepared before you take your hiatus.

The most important thing is to record all the work you've done prior to your time off. You have to be your own archivist. You have to document your own career, and you need your supervisors to sign off and verify your accomplishments. It's a mistake to think you can go back to someone, years later, and expect them to remember everything you did.

Before taking extended family leave, sit down with your supervisor. Ask him or her to itemize the work you've done over the past year, as well as your professional skill sets. If you're not planning to leave the company permanently, ask that the document be added to your personnel file. Also be sure to keep a copy for yourself—just in case your plans change in the future. When you are ready to return to work, this document will help validate your accomplishments and abilities with your future employer.

Outside of documentation, the best thing you can do is network. Before you leave your job, reach out to your own network and give them a short status update. You don't need to go into any uncomfortable specifics. Just let them know you're taking some extended time off, and that you plan on returning in the future. The purpose here is to keep your network informed of your status and your intent.

When you're planning to return to work, reach out to your network again and ask about any possible openings. Also think about how you can access your network's networks. Indeed, second- and third-degree contacts are sometimes the most fruitful relationships when it comes to uncovering new opportunities. Even relatively weak connections can open doors for you.

Consider a portfolio career. As noted previously, many experts view job security as an outmoded concept. A truly risk-free career comes from knowing that your skills are marketable and transferable to a variety of projects and positions. In Chapter 7 we discussed self-employment and how many people put together different projects to create a career or business. Combinations of projects like these are often referred to as a portfolio career.

- **What is a portfolio career?** In its simplest form, a portfolio career is one that allows you to combine a variety of projects, paid and unpaid, to create full-time work for yourself that may be more meaningful than a single full-time job with just one employer. Examples of activities that can be part of a portfolio career are part-time jobs, freelance projects, temporary jobs, contract positions, volunteer opportunities, and full-time self-employment.

- **When should I consider a portfolio career?** Laura Schlafly, founder of Life Choices with Laura and coauthor with Dr. Deepak Chopra of *Roadmap to Success*, writes about portfolio careers and midlife job seekers. She suggests considering a portfolio career in the following situations:

  - if you're frustrated with your current employer.

  - if you're starting your career.

  - if you're seeking less stressful work.

- if you're self-employed or starting your own business.

- if you're unemployed and need paid work.

- if you're retired but would like to keep working at a paying job.

- if you're balancing other responsibilities but want paid work.

- **What are the benefits of a portfolio career?** For people who are self-motivated, energetic, and not afraid of risk, a portfolio career is a good option for the following reasons. It is the best way to diffuse employment risk while diversifying your sources of income. The flexibility that comes from stepping outside the nine-to-five routine gives you more options and more freedom. You learn the value of your skills in the market and are able to put a price tag on them. There is the excitement that comes from moving from one engaging project to the next. And you may feel more ownership and emotional investment in your projects when you are working for yourself.

- **What is the downside to a portfolio career?** As with full-time self-employment, portfolio careers are a good fit for people who manage time well and are multitaskers. People who like structure, routine, and hierarchy may find a portfolio career difficult to sustain emotionally. Its disadvantages include a certain amount of financial risk, the potential for stress when deadlines collide, and uncertainty about what is coming down the line tomorrow, next week, next month, and next year.

- **What strategies do I need to create a successful portfolio career?** If you decide a portfolio career is right for you, Laura suggests considering the following options and ideas to help ease the way:

  - Build at least six months of savings to support any startup costs. Not even high-wire aerialists like working without a net.

  - Take a starter position in one or more of your areas of interest. This allows you to earn some income while learning and exploring. There is no need to stay too long in any one role or company. This is a valuable baby step and works especially well for folks who have lower living costs and can afford the risk.

  - Work part time in your current job or field to cover your basic living costs, such as your rent or mortgage. Then focus your remaining time in real portfolio research. Take this time to try on your possibilities and find out what fits.

  - Throw caution to the wind and take the leap. Risky? You bet, especially if you have dependents. So you'll probably feel more at ease if you also create a Plan B to turn to if at first you don't succeed. This all-or-nothing approach requires laser focus and abundant self-motivation in addition to knowing your dependable strengths—those natural talents you have.

- Make sure you have the support you need. That means emotional support from family, friends, and colleagues; developmental support from peers such as mentors or career experts; promotional support from people who will share their connections and introduce you to key people in your field; and material support from service providers and financiers as needed.

Don't ever stop learning.

According to the Pew Research Center, 63% of U.S. workers are considered professional learners. This means that they have gotten some kind of extra professional training over the last year, either related to career growth or job insecurity. Of those professional learners, 65% say that learning expanded their professional network and 47% say it helped them advance within their current company.

Many people find satisfaction in lifelong learning and keeping their study and research skills current. Whether you are drawn to courses that are related to your current profession or to content in new areas, it can be exciting, interesting, and mind-opening to explore different ideas and viewpoints. Try to take advantage of all the opportunities for learning that present themselves.

Decide whether graduate school is right for you. As mentioned previously, today's economy is more focused on skills and results than on academic credentials and degrees. Yet in some cases, the decision to go to graduate school can reap a wide variety of benefits, both for you as an individual and for your long-term career path as well.

Answer these questions before deciding to apply. Consider the following before you decide to invest your precious time and money in the pursuit of a graduate degree:

- **Do you want to switch fields?** Getting a degree may be the only path to that new career, or it may be a big shortcut to years of piecing together relevant work experience. Informational interviews with connections in your desired field can help you decide whether going back to school is necessary.

- **What is needed for promotion and job security in your field?** In certain careers, advancement and growth are not possible without additional certification, training, degrees, or licenses. Continuing education can pave the way for advancement by giving you new skills and keeping you informed of new trends in your industry. It can also pave a path for a different job or a promotion.

- **Is it worth the time commitment?** It's always better financially for you to get your degree while still working, but that requires a lot of juggling and a fair amount of lost sleep. Do some soul-searching, evaluate your available time, look at your financial situation, and assess whether you can afford to go to graduate school full or part time. Ask yourself, "Is the long-term benefit worth the sacrifices I'll be making?" It is important to evaluate the costs of going back to school and the potential return on your investment.

Know how graduate school can help you. If you decide to go, here are a few of the benefits you can expect to receive.

- **Updated skills:** Your writing improves dramatically when faced with the red pen marks of a professor. You'll also make dozens of presentations, which will boost your public speaking skills. Finally, you'll gain confidence from being surrounded by peers in your field and sharing information and ideas with them.

- **A knowledge of new trends:** Any program worth its salt is doing everything it can to keep ahead of the trends and to train its students to be innovators in the field. You'll likely attend workshops led by top minds and local leaders in your field as part of your program's courses and extracurricular events.

- **An expanded professional network:** You'll meet many people in the community doing great work in your chosen field. Build relationships, connect on LinkedIn, meet for coffee to discuss shared interests; whatever you do, leverage relationships with your classmates, your professors, and guest speakers. It will pay off.

Consider local alternatives to graduate school. Maybe you just need a few courses to add or brush up on skills or some additional training to show you've mastered a specific skill set. Here are some areas to explore instead of undertaking a complete graduate school program.

- **Professional certificates:** At the Career One Stop Certification Center, sponsored by the U.S. Department of Labor, the Certification Finder search tool helps you locate certification options in a variety of careers, occupations, and industries.

- **Professional workshops, credentials, and endorsements:** Seek out some of the many options that exist in this area. For example, the Nonprofit Leadership Alliance offers a Certified Nonprofit Professional (CNP) credential to students who are seeking careers in nonprofit management. The Society of Professional Journalists offers a variety of training options for those interested in a career in journalism, while The Art Institutes offer college-bound courses as well as non-credentialed courses in the design, media arts, fashion, and culinary fields.

- **Community courses:** Community colleges offer a wide range of classes from how to use Excel to grant writing at an affordable cost. They are a great way to explore new content fields without a major commitment of time or money.

Follow these blogs! The following are some of our favorite job-related blogs here at Mac's List. Some have been referenced in other chapters, but here they are in one neat and tidy package.

- **All Groan Up**: Paul Angone offers career and life advice to millennials in his thoughtful and humorous blog.

- **Ask a Manager:** Before striking out as a consultant, Alison Green was chief of staff for a medium-sized organization. Every day she answers questions about workplace and job-search topics.

- **InternMatch**: Jenny Xie posts several times a week about topics of interest to interns and college students, including tips about landing internships and making the most of them. The InternMatch site includes hundreds of internship openings across the country.

- **Jobhuntercoach**: Arnie Fertig lives in New England where he ran his own recruiting company for ten years. He now helps people master the skills they need for focused job searches and shares what he learned as a recruiter via weekly blog posts.

- **Kontrary**: Rebecca Healy blogs from Washington, DC, on how to navigate your career, money, and life so that "you can find meaningful work, enjoy the heck out of it, and earn more money."

- **Life After College**: Jenny Blake is an author and career and business coach in New York City. A former Google employee, Jenny and her team write about life, careers, goals, and relationships with a special focus on issues of interest to twenty-somethings.
- **Penelope Trunk**: A founder of Brazen Careerist, a career site for professionals, Penelope writes regularly about career management and job-search issues of interest to Generation Y.

And don't forget these blogs by some of our career experts! ! Many of them write their own blogs and/or contribute frequently to others' blogs.

- **Career Enlightenment**: Social media expert Joshua Waldman writes for job seekers looking for comprehensive information about conducting a job search online.
- **Pathfinder Writing and Career Services**: Speaker, author, and resume writer Dawn Rasmussen's blog offers ideas and tools people can use to manage their careers and find fulfilling jobs.
- **Kerry Hannon**: Kerry's blog is full of great job search and career advice for workers of all ages.
- **JobJenny**: Jenny Foss is a career strategist and the voice of the popular career blog JobJenny.com. Jenny also operates an agency and is the author of the Ridiculously Awesome Resume Kit and the Ridiculously Awesome LinkedIn Kit.
- **Coaching for Clarity**: Aubrie De Clerck helps you open doors to fulfilling work.
- **Career Factors**: Founder of Career Factors, Marsha Warner, SPHR, is an executive recruiter and career coach. She teaches groups, works individually with clients in career transition, speaks at local job-search groups, and has published on the topics of career management, recruiting, and career renewal.

Dig deeper!

For links to some of the topics covered in this chapter (including getting unstuck, professional workshops, the changing job market, and the role of hobbies in a job search), go to www.macslist.org/references.

You've reached

The End

of our book but we are confident
that with what you've learned
you'll shortly be starting on

The Beginning

of a great new job!
Good luck and let us know how it goes!
(Please use the following few pages for notes.)

The Mac's List Team
mac@macslist.org

ISBN: 978-0-9909551-3-9

*"The most difficult thing is the decision to act;
the rest is merely tenacity."*

Amelia Earhart

"One important key to success is self-confidence.
An important key to self-confidence is preparation."

Arthur Ashe

_____

_____

_____

_____

_____

_____

_____

_____

_____

_____

_____

_____

_____

_____

_____

_____

_____

_____

"I was once afraid of people saying, 'Who does she think she is?' Now I have the courage to stand and say, 'This is who I am.'"

Oprah Winfrey

If you're going through hell, keep going."

Winston Churchill

_____

_____

_____

_____

_____

_____

_____

_____

_____

_____

_____

_____

_____

_____

_____

_____

_____

_____

_____

_____

Notes

Build a magnetic professional brand with our free online course!

At least 80% of employers use internet searches to screen job candidates. What do they see when they Google your name?

A polished, accomplished professional? Or pictures from your wild weekend in Vegas?

How to Wow and Woo Employers Online is a free course that teaches you everything you need to build an internet presence that captures employers' attention—for the right reasons.

You'll learn how to:

- edit, delete, or bury questionable content that shows up on search engines and social media.

- craft a LinkedIn profile that attracts hiring managers and recruiters.

- use Twitter to build your online brand and find great jobs.

Register for this FREE online course at **macslist.org/woo**.